T0068033

The Three-Petalled Rose

How the Synthesis of Judaism, Buddhism, and Stoicism
Can Create a Healthy, Fulfilled and Flourishing Life

Ronald W. Pies MD

iUniverse, Inc.
Bloomington

The Three-Petalled Rose
How the Synthesis of Judaism, Buddhism, and Stoicism
Can Create a Healthy, Fulfilled and Flourishing Life

Copyright © 2013 by Ronald W. Pies MD.

All rights reserved. No part of this book may be used or reproduced by any means, graphic, electronic, or mechanical, including photocopying, recording, taping or by any information storage retrieval system without the written permission of the publisher except in the case of brief quotations embodied in critical articles and reviews.

iUniverse books may be ordered through booksellers or by contacting:

iUniverse
1663 Liberty Drive
Bloomington, IN 47403
www.iuniverse.com
1-800-Authors (1-800-288-4677)

Because of the dynamic nature of the Internet, any web addresses or links contained in this book may have changed since publication and may no longer be valid. The views expressed in this work are solely those of the author and do not necessarily reflect the views of the publisher, and the publisher hereby disclaims any responsibility for them.

Any people depicted in stock imagery provided by Thinkstock are models, and such images are being used for illustrative purposes only.
Certain stock imagery © Thinkstock.

ISBN: 978-1-4759-7156-9 (sc)
ISBN: 978-1-4759-7157-6 (ebk)

Printed in the United States of America

iUniverse rev. date: 01/24/2013

Table of Contents

Acknowledgments

I would like to thank Cynthia M.A. Geppert MD, PhD, for her careful safeguarding of earlier drafts of this work, as well as for her guidance in ethical and spiritual matters over the years. I would also like to thank Prof. Stephen Prothero, for his helpful referral information; and in particular, Mr. Connor Wood, MTS, for his astute comments and suggestions on chapter 1. Numerous lectures on eastern religion by Prof. Stephen Prothero and Prof. Jay Garfield have been enormously helpful in formulating many of my ideas. I also thank Prof. Damien Keown for his helpful guidance on Buddhist texts.

Introduction

This is a book for anyone who wants to live "the good life," but who has not yet found a clear path to that goal. Of course, what is "right" for one person may not be right for another, and the path I chart in this book may not be the best one for you. In my own spiritual journey, over the past 50 or so years, I have found a good deal of wisdom in all the major religious and spiritual traditions—and also in the writings of individuals who have no religious or spiritual inclinations at all. (There are, after all, many wise and humane agnostics and atheists—some of whom have more helpful things to say about "the good life" than many theologians!). That great repository of Jewish wisdom, the Talmud, asks, "Who is wise?" and answers, "The one who learns from all people." I have tried to keep this in mind, even as I have focused on three particular spiritual traditions: Judaism, Buddhism, and Stoicism.

When I first embarked on writing this, the title I had in mind was "JuBuSto: A Synthesis of Judaism, Buddhism and Stoicism." Eventually, I decided that "JuBuSto" was an odd-sounding neologism, and settled on "The Three-Petalled Rose." This title, as some readers may recognize, is a respectful nod to Rabbi Adin Steinsaltz's classic, *The Thirteen-Petalled Rose*, with no claim to have reached the exalted heights of that work. Indeed, I present this book with an important caveat: I am a psychiatric physician by training, not a religious scholar, rabbi, monk, or theologian. In fact, I came rather late to any spiritual path, having spent much of my youth rebelling against my Jewish roots and upbringing! But for the past twenty-five years or so, I have had the opportunity to study several of the major faiths, and to integrate some of their psychological wisdom into my own life. Most of my studies have involved independent reading, though I was privileged to receive some valuable instruction from Rabbi David Lerner, Rabbi Jack Bemporad, and Rabbi Dr. Ruth Sandberg.

As a psychiatrist, I was of course trained in several schools of psychotherapy, but I became especially fascinated with cognitive-behavioral therapy. (CBT). This approach emphasizes the importance of rational and logical thinking in the attainment of mental health. Unlike psychoanalytic forms of therapy, CBT does not emphasize unconscious conflicts and repressed memories; rather, it focuses on the "here-and-now" beliefs and behaviors of the individual. The psychiatrist Aaron Beck and the psychologist Albert Ellis were especially strong influences on me, both as a mental health professional and as a person seeking solace, wisdom, and happiness. Ellis was, arguably, the first clinician to develop a cognitively-oriented form of therapy—ultimately termed REBT (Rational emotive behavior therapy). Ellis's work shaped and informed Aaron Beck's work, which evolved in its own way over the years. My late mother, Frances Pies Oliver, was a protégée of Albert Ellis and first introduced me to his ideas when I was still in my adolescence—for which, to this day, I remain immensely grateful to her.

What do CBT and REBT have to do with Judaism, Buddhism, and Stoicism? Well, a great deal, as it turns out. Like these very secular schools of psychotherapy, the three spiritual traditions share a foundational value that permeates nearly all their core teachings; namely, the importance of *thinking clearly*. Of course, each tradition has a somewhat different take on what "thinking clearly" means—and, in some forms of Zen Buddhism, "thinking" plays a decidedly smaller role than that of direct experience, meditation, or sudden flashes of insight. The same may be said for the more mystical branch of Judaism, known as *Hasidism*. Even the highly intellectual Stoic tradition is not always focused on logic and rational thinking. There is a spiritual, even a mystical, dimension to Stoicism that is rarely recognized today. And yet, I would argue that all three traditions share with CBT and REBT the following basic tenet: our happiness and fulfillment in life is critically dependent on *the quality of our thinking*. In effect, we create our own happiness by thinking "good" thoughts—and produce our own misery by filling our minds with "bad" thoughts! As the Thai Buddhist Master Ajahn Chah (1918-92) put it,

> "We want to be free of suffering . . . but still we
> suffer. Why is this? It's because of wrong thinking. If
> our thinking is in harmony with the way things are,
> we will have well-being."

Indeed, the concept of living in harmony with Nature—and accepting things as they are—is crucial to both Buddhism and Stoicism. A modified version of this idea also appears in some strains of Judaism, though in traditional Judaism living in harmony with *God's law* is the critical requirement. More broadly, however, all three spiritual paths emphasize that we often sabotage our own chances for living the "good life." As one great Buddhist sage, Santideva (7th c. AD), put it in a famous lecture:

> "Eager to escape sorrow, men rush into sorrow;
> from desire of happiness, they blindly slay their own
> happiness, enemies to themselves."

This leads us to the crucial *ethical* dimension to all three of the traditions I discuss. I don't mean simply that Judaism, Buddhism, and Stoicism stress ethical behavior, though they certainly do. I mean that, for each of these traditions, *ethical conduct is the key to a fulfilled and flourishing life*. Does this mean that ethical conduct is the key to "happiness?" Well, that term doesn't do justice to what is being described here. Perhaps the Greek term *eudaimonia* comes closest to expressing the concept of a "flourishing life."

The term is derived from the prefix *eu*—meaning "good"—and *daimon*, meaning "spirit" As the Greek philosopher, Aristotle, used the term, *eudaimonia* was much more than a fleeting feeling of happiness or pleasure, such as we might get from a good meal or a relaxing massage! For Aristotle, the "flourishing life" consisted in *using our rational faculties in accordance with virtue*. The key word is "using," with the implication that the flourishing life must involve *action*—not just sitting around thinking virtuous thoughts! (The English statesman Benjamin Disraeli put it well: "Action may not always bring happiness; but there is no happiness without action.")

The Stoics were even more insistent than Aristotle that the virtuous life is the very core of *eudaimonia*. Now, doing the "right thing" doesn't always lead to immediate pleasure, as anybody who has paid income taxes knows. Yet all three spiritual traditions—Judaism, Buddhism, and Stoicism—assert that we become truly and deeply fulfilled as human beings *only through virtuous action*.

There are, of course, many religious aspects of these three traditions—particularly in Judaism—that can't be reduced to "secular wisdom" or cognitive strategies. It would be foolish and misleading to pretend otherwise. It would also be wrong to suggest that these three spiritual traditions are cut from the same theological cloth, and that we can easily "mix and match" aspects of one with the other two. In some respects, for example, Buddhism and Judaism reach quite different conclusions about how to attain "the good life." As a general rule, Buddhism is not a "God-based" belief system—or arguably, even a "belief system" at all. It is more an orientation or "attitude" toward life, and a set of *practices* aimed at freeing the individual from misery and delusion. (That said, some forms of Buddhism do involve "deities" of one form or another—more on this later). In contrast, Judaism is almost impossible to separate from the concept of God, at least historically and traditionally. As Holocaust survivor, philosopher, and writer, Elie Wiesel has said: "You can be a Jew with God. You can be a Jew against God. But not without God."

And yet, these distinguishing features of Buddhism and Judaism are only rough generalizations, as we'll soon see. There are some Buddhists who seem to regard the Buddha as a kind of deity; and, there are many individuals who consider themselves Jews, but who do not believe in the God of the Old Testament or, indeed, any god at all. Rather, they see themselves as the heirs to an ethical and cultural tradition, in which the individual's obligation is to promote certain humane values. And while many scholars of Judaism deny the claim that Buddhism and Judaism are "compatible," many spiritually inclined individuals would beg to differ. Indeed, in the Urban Dictionary, we find the slightly disparaging term "BuJew" to describe a "Buddhist Jew." The idea that Judaism and Buddhism may be compatible on some level was made famous in Rodger Kamenetz's popular book, *The Jew in the Lotus*. One review of this book noted how it revealed ". . . the intricate inner lives of the Jewish Buddhists who cross forbidden lines, obliterate distinctions, [and] insist they can be more than one thing at a time without loss." (Rosellen Brown). Theologians may cry out in protest at this kind of synthesis, but in my view, there are psychological and ethical elements of Judaism and Buddhism that *can* be harmonized. And both these spiritual traditions have much in common with Stoic ethics and psychology.

A word on the structure of most chapters in this book: I will usually begin with some key quotations from various "masters" within the three traditions. This will generally be followed by a thematic vignette, representing the spiritual "problem" addressed in the chapter. These vignettes are "composites", based in part on patients I have treated, as well as some individuals I have known. For example, I might describe an everyday, 21st-century housewife or parent, trying to cope with feelings of guilt or inadequacy. In some cases, I then provide an "analysis" of the person's problem from the viewpoint of the three spiritual traditions. In other cases, the personal vignette serves mainly to illustrate points in the discussions that follow, which may allude to some key themes in the vignette. Finally, I present my own "synthesis" of the wisdom gleaned from all three spiritual paths, sometimes incorporating insights from the cognitive-behavioral sciences, and various literary or philosophical sources. I hope that by using modern-day examples, I'll be able to show you that the spiritual issues raised two thousand years ago are still vibrantly alive and relevant today. The reader will notice that there is some repetition and considerable "overlap" in the material, moving from chapter to chapter—a consequence of the fluid boundaries between categories such as "The Common Bond of Humanity" and "Ethical Obligations and the Flourishing Life." It's fair to say that each of the chapter headings is merely one facet of the same "jewel"—and thus likely to reflect very similar values.

No scholarly expertise or special knowledge of religion is required to understand this book; nor is any belief in such Hindu and Buddhist concepts as *karma*, *samsara*, reincarnation, etc. (We'll explore the meaning of these terms shortly). Similarly, the reader need have no belief in a "supreme being" or any allegiance to the theological or metaphysical claims of Judaism or Stoicism. All you need is an open mind and a sincere desire to create an "awakened" and flourishing life.

Finally, a word on the title, *The Three-Petalled Rose*. Readers may be reminded of the famous work on Jewish mysticism, *The Thirteen-Petalled Rose*, by the renowned Talmudic scholar Rabbi Adin Steinsaltz. But I certainly make no claim to match Rabbi Steinsaltz's scholarship, or his understanding of Jewish mysticism. This book, rather, is intended as a practical guide to character development, as a means of achieving the "flourishing life." As the religious educator Catherine Beyer has noted, the rose is linked, symbolically, with the transformation of food from the soil into a beautiful, fragrant flower. My hope is that the reader will take the spiritual "nutrients" from the three ancient traditions of Judaism, Buddhism, and Stoicism, and transform them into a life of beauty, order, and purpose.

*   *   *

Note: I do not distinguish between Pali and Sanskrit spellings of most terms in the Buddhist literature, since most introductory texts on Buddhism use both forms; e.g., *dhamma* in Pali, or *dharma* in Sanskrit.

Chapter 1

AN OVERVIEW OF JUDAISM, BUDDHISM, STOICISM

A Little Orientation First

It's not easy to summarize three ancient and complex spiritual traditions without leaving out a lot of important material. But, before we begin exploring how Judaism, Buddhism, and Stoicism can help us live fulfilling lives, we need to get a basic idea of what these traditions claim and teach. Of the three, Judaism is by far the oldest, if we consider the age of the oldest documents composing the so-called Old Testament—sometimes called "The Hebrew Bible." It's thought that these scriptures date to at least the 7th century B.C. (which historians now call "B.C.E."—Before the Common Era). The biblical scholar William M. Schniedewind believes that the Book of Deuteronomy was probably compiled around that time, and that composition of other portions of the Old Testament continued into the 6th century BCE. However, the great storehouse of rabbinical commentary on the Hebrew Bible—known as the *Talmud*—was not assembled and edited until roughly the second century AD (called "C.E." or "Common Era" by historians), under the direction of Rabbi Judah ha-Nasi.

Most historians believe that the man who would be called "the Buddha"—Siddhartha Gautama—lived from roughly 560 BCE

1

to around 480 BCE—perhaps a century or two after the Hebrew Bible began to be compiled. His oral teachings were probably not compiled in written form until several centuries later. And finally, the Stoic philosophers did not enter the scene until around the 3rd century BCE, when Zeno of Citium began teaching in the Greek city of Athens—a relative newcomer! And so, in deference to its seniority, we'll begin our discussion with a brief synopsis of Judaism, focusing especially on Talmudic Judaism.

Judaism: A Whirlwind Tour of Its Core Texts, Beliefs, and Values

Some consider Judaism a religion. Some consider it a "culture," a "nation" (as in "the People of Israel"), an ethnic identity, or a set of ethical principles. Most scholars would argue that Judaism has elements of *all* these descriptions, and that the totality of Judaism (and the Jewish people) is greater than the sum of its parts. As Prof. Jon D. Levenson has observed, "When it comes to the Jewish people, our convenient categories fail us."

By some lights, Judaism is the world's oldest religious tradition, though some would argue that the early roots of Hinduism go back at least as far—perhaps to the second millennium before the birth of Jesus. In any case, there is little question that Judaism is the oldest *monotheistic* religion. Indeed, the words "Hear, O Israel, the Lord is our God, the Lord is One"—found in the prayer called the *Sh'ma*—are often considered the very foundation of traditional Judaism. As Rabbi Hayim H. Donin has observed, the underlying faith of the Jewish people has been the belief in ". . . one, indivisible God, by whose will the universe and all that is in it was created." That said, this "orthodox" view has been buffeted by the winds of revision and reconsideration in recent times. For example, we now find many who identify themselves as

"Jews," but who do not subscribe to the traditional monotheistic position—or even to the notion that there is a superhuman being called "God." For example, "Humanistic Judaism"—founded in 1963 by Rabbi Sherwin Wine—is a non-theistic philosophy that embraces Jewish culture, values, and ideas. As we'll see, some of these secularly inclined individuals find it possible to identify with the Jewish people, and yet also to embrace elements of Buddhism or other faiths.

Nevertheless, we need to begin by discussing the traditional cornerstones of Judaism. It's fair to say that the *ethics* of Judaism rests atop two gigantic pillars: the *Torah* and the *Talmud.* The word "Torah" is often translated as "Law," but that term is somewhat inaccurate. "Torah" is derived from the Hebrew *yarah,* meaning "to indicate" or "to instruct." So, on one level, Torah is essentially the entire body of ethical "instruction" that guides the Jewish people. More concretely, however, *Torah* is usually the name given to the Five Books of Moses (also called the *"Pentateuch"*). Most of us know these books by the names *Genesis, Exodus, Leviticus, Numbers,* and *Deuteronomy*—the first five books of the Hebrew Bible. The term "Torah" is also applied more broadly to the five books of Moses; the eight books of the *prophets*; and the eleven books of *writings*. Together, these 24 books make up the written law, known collectively as *Tanakh*—an acronym formed from letters in the Hebrew words *T*orah, *N*evi'im ("Prophets"), and *K*etuvim ("Writings").

On a more mystical level, Torah is sometimes viewed as the underlying moral structure of the entire Universe. In fact, rabbinical teaching holds that the Torah actually preceded the creation of the world, and that God himself was guided by it! You might imagine that, for the Jewish people, no text or teaching could ever surpass Torah, or even complement it in any way. In a sense this is true—nothing is "higher" than Torah. But the ancient rabbis knew that the Torah—often vague on many details—required a kind of "user's manual" to show people how to live practically by its commandments. And here we enter the world of *Talmud.*

The Talmud arose in the context of destruction and rebirth. In the year 70 CE (AD), the Romans destroyed the ancient Temple in Jerusalem. Though a devastating blow to the Jewish people, this catastrophe actually gave birth to what we know as "rabbinical Judaism". Rather than focusing on sacrifice and worship in the Temple, the energies of the Jews shifted to new centers of learning, where scholars assembled fragments of the ancient, oral tradition into a coherent, written form—the Talmud.

This very lengthy compilation of rabbinical commentaries on the Torah consists of two parts, called the *Mishnah* and the *Gemara.* Just as the *Mishnah* comments on the Torah, the *Gemara* comments on the *Mishnah.* The Talmud contains both legal (*halachic*) and non-legal (*aggadic*) material—though in Jewish tradition, the two are often closely interwoven. Basically, *halacha* details what Jews are required to do, or are prohibited from doing; *aggadah* consists mainly of stories, homilies and rabbinical teachings that put Jewish law into a "human", ethical context. The Aggadic material is of special interest to us, since many of the purely ethical teachings of the Talmud are contained in its Aggadic portions. Undoubtedly the best-known of these is *Pirke Avot*, sometimes translated as "Chapters of the Sages" or "Ethics of the Fathers." *Pirke Avot* is the only book of the Talmud that deals exclusively with the moral and ethical lessons of the Sages.

By now, you may have concluded that Torah and Talmud are really texts meant only for Jews—but that would be a distinctly "un-Jewish" conclusion! The philosopher Rabbi Leo Baeck (1873-1956) pointed out that nowhere in the Hebrew Bible or later rabbinical writings does the term "good Jew" occur. Rather, it is the "good man" (and good woman) who is the object of ethical concern—the individual we often call a *mensch.*

Is it possible to summarize the main ethical values of rabbinical and Talmudic Judaism? At the risk of drastically oversimplifying, it is reasonable to regard *the pursuit of truth, peace, justice, and loving-kindness (mercy and compassion)* as preeminent Jewish values. However, as Rabbi Jack Bemporad has pointed out, it is really the *sanctification of life* that underlies and animates these values, and serves as the keystone in the great arch of Jewish ethics. In addition, the following values are also central to the Jewish tradition:

- Generosity and charity
- Self-mastery and self-discipline
- Moderation and adhering to "The Middle Way"
- Humility and flexibility
- Forgiveness and willingness to make apology
- Respect for self and others
- Attentive listening
- Acquiring knowledge and wisdom
- Caution and prudence
- Discussing and criticizing others fairly
- Trustworthiness and fidelity
- Gratitude and contentedness with one's lot
- Politeness and tact
- Honoring and revering parents and teachers

We'll cover many of these values in the course of this book. But we can begin by citing perhaps the most famous—and possibly, the most brilliant—synopsis of Jewish ethics, attributed to the first-century C.E. sage Hillel the Elder. Legend has it that the renowned teacher was asked by a non-believer to teach him the entire Torah while he, the non-Jew, stood on one foot! Without becoming angry at this provocation, Hillel replied simply, "That which is hateful to you, do not do to your fellow.

That is the whole Torah, the rest is commentary; now go and learn." When joined to the closely related concept of *kindness and compassion*—in Hebrew, *rahamim*—Hillel's teaching may truly be considered the heart and soul of Judaic ethics.

Judaism does not see mankind as inherently good or evil, or tainted by "original sin" as Paul the Apostle asserts in the New Testament. Rather, Judaism stresses that while we are all made in "the image of God," each of us has the potential for doing both good *and* evil. Each of us must struggle with both our "good impulse" (called *yetzer hatov*) and our "evil impulse" (called *yetzer hara*). That said—while human beings are not born with "original sin"—the rabbis of the Talmud *did* give the "evil impulse" a slight edge: compared with the "good impulse", the *yetzer hara* is thirteen years older and somewhat stronger!

Yet the rabbis showed tremendous psychological sophistication in this regard. They recognized that within the so-called "evil impulse" are found the seeds of good. There is a saying in the Talmud to the effect that, without our *yetzer hara*, we wouldn't bother to marry, or even to build a house. This may seem puzzling at first—what does marriage or building a house have to do with the evil impulse? But many psychologists understand that these activities require a certain *willingness to take a risk*, and to overcome the temptation to retreat into isolation or apathy.

There is an element of "ego" that is required to take such risks—and maybe a little "chutzpah" (roughly, "nerve") as well! Carried to an extreme, "ego" can become megalomania. But when the ego is guided by wisdom and compassion, good things may come of it. Thus, there is a sense in which the *yetzer hara* might be called "the creative urge" rather than "the evil impulse." In this sense, *yetzer hara* has affinities with Freud's concept of *Eros*, or "life instinct." Talmudic scholar Jeffrey Spitzer has expressed this concept well. He writes,

> "*Yetzer hara* is not a demonic force that pushes a
> person to do evil, but rather a drive toward pleasure
> or property or security, which if left unlimited, can
> lead to evil (cf. Genesis Rabbah 9:7). When properly
> controlled by the yetzer hatov, the yetzer hara leads to
> many socially desirable results, including marriage,
> business, and community." [myjewishlearning.com]

In short, Judaism does not require us to renounce or root
out our *yetzer hara*—rather, we are required to shape and restrain
it—and to *use it in the service of higher aims and purposes.*

Most important, Judaism regards each of us as *free to choose*
between our good and evil impulses: we are not, as in Calvinism,
"predestined" to one fate or another. In the words of *Pirke Avot*
(3:19), "Everything is foreseen [by God], yet free will is given."

*   *   *

Judaism brings far more to the spiritual table than its
religious and ethical values, though these are, of course, of central
importance. I believe rabbinical and Talmudic Judaism is filled
with psychological insights of unsurpassed subtlety and wisdom.
These insights, as I'll try to show, may help guide us in our quest
for "the good life." For example, Judaism recognizes that *our
greatest strength is our ability to master ourselves; that we rarely if
ever succeed in reaching all our goals or satisfying their desires; that
even in the face of our personal shortcomings, we must not condemn
ourselves; and that while belief in oneself is important, it is not
enough.* Thus, we find rabbinical teachings such as these:

> "Ben Zoma says: Who is mighty? One who
> conquers one's passions . . . [and] one who rules over

one's spirit is better than one who conquers a city."
[Pirke Avot 4:1]

"No one ever leaves this world with even half his
desires fulfilled." [commentary on Ecclesiastes,
Midrash]

Rabbi Shimon says . . . "do not consider yourself
wicked." [Pirke Avot 2:18]

He [Hillel the Elder] used to say, "If I am not for
myself, who is for me? When I am for myself alone,
what am I? And if not now, when?" [Pirke Avot 1;14]

With that introduction, let's take a very brief tour of the
psychological and interpersonal territory within the literature
of rabbinical Judaism, which we'll explore in more detail in
later chapters. In this, and in our subsequent discussion of the
Buddhism and Stoicism, I will focus on *four key areas* bearing on
human thought, feeling, and conduct.

• Tact, Empathy, and Compassion

The Judaic tradition places great emphasis on consideration
for the feelings and sensitivities of others. In *Pirke Avot*, we are
admonished that "The wise man does not speak before one who is
wiser than him and does not break into the words of another . . ."
and that "A fence for wisdom is silence . . ." We are taught the
importance not only of holding our peace, but also of "timing"
our comments so as to avoid bruised feelings. This is especially
important in our dealings with the angry, the distraught, and the
bereaved. Thus, we are told,

"Do not appease your fellow at the time of his anger, do not console him at the time his dead lies before him . . . [and] do not attempt to see him at the time of his downfall." [*Pirke Avot*]. Recognizing that our good intentions are not enough, another portion of the Talmud adds, "Don't console a mourner after he has visibly consoled himself."

And finally, the Rabbis of the Talmud were adamant in their condemnation of shaming another human being. They recognized what almost every psychologist today would affirm: "Humiliation is worse than physical pain." Indeed, the rabbis believed that "Whoever shames another in public is like one who sheds blood." (This last comment may have been based on the astute observation that the person publicly shamed does not blush—rather, he *blanches*, as the blood leaves his face).

• **Anger, Rage, and Revenge**

The rabbis of the Talmud had a deep understanding of the destructive force of anger. With very few exceptions, they believed that anger, rage, and vengeance were always to be avoided, and that our failing to do so is often the beginning of our ruin. The Talmud warns that "The person who loses his temper forgets his learning, and . . . gradually becomes more and more foolish." "Anger," the rabbis continue, "deprives the sage of his wisdom, [and] a prophet of his vision." Yet the rabbis understood how difficult it is to suppress our anger, much less not to feel it in the first place. Indeed, the Talmud tells us that God Himself prays that He will constrain his wrath! God says, 'May it be My will that My mercy may suppress My anger, and that My mercy may prevail over My [other] attributes, so that I may deal with My children in the attribute of mercy . . .'

The sages of the Talmud seem almost prescient in their understanding of psychosomatic symptoms. For example, we know today that intense and prolonged anger can take its toll on our health, contributing to a variety of illnesses. Rabbi Samuel ben Nahmani said as much in the Talmud, nearly two millennia ago. "Remove anger from your heart," he tells us, and "thus wilt you put away evil from your flesh . . ." for the angry person ". . . is made to suffer from abdominal troubles . . . a trembling heart . . . failing of eyes, and sorrow of mind." (We are put in mind of a quote attributed to the Buddha, Siddhartha Gautama: "The grudge you hold on to is like a hot coal that you intend to throw at someone, only you're the one who gets burned!"). The rabbis were also well aware that the angry person is tempted to avenge the perceived injustice or insult by lashing out at the perpetrator. Yet the sages counseled a higher path: "How shall a person take revenge of his enemy? Let him add new virtues to himself." (Here, we are put in mind of the Stoic philosopher-emperor, Marcus Aurelius (121-180 CE), who counseled, "The best revenge is not to become like the one who wronged you.").

• Worry, Sorrow, and Depression

The Rabbis of the Talmud had plenty to worry about, and many reasons for sorrow. After all, as we observed earlier, the Talmudic era followed the destruction of the Temple in Jerusalem This cataclysm actually followed a failed revolt by the Jews against their Roman oppressors. This was also a time in which the Jews were divided against themselves, with a group known as the Zealots favoring rebellion against Rome, and many less radical Jewish leaders opposing it. Tragically, Zealot rebels often killed Jewish leaders who didn't fully support their revolt.

Given this backdrop, it's understandable that the rabbis had a somewhat ambivalent attitude toward "worrying." On the one hand, the Talmud tells us, "Do not worry about tomorrow's trouble, for you never know what the day will bring." So far, so good. But the commentator then adds, "Maybe by the time tomorrow arrives you won't be here anymore, and you worried about a world that was not yours." Perhaps this is not the most comforting thought for many of us! Nevertheless, the rabbis were well aware of the corrosive effect worry can have on the mind and body. Once again, the Talmud seems to have anticipated findings of modern psychosomatic medicine when it tells us, "Worry can kill; therefore let not anxiety enter your heart, for it has slain many a person." (We now know that, indeed, there is an increased risk of fatal coronary heart disease among patients with panic disorder, phobic anxiety, and other anxiety disorders).

The rabbis also understood the profound depths into which the soul can sink after the loss of a loved one. Thus, the Talmud observes, "For a man whose wife had died during his lifetime, the world is steeped in darkness . . . His steps become short . . . His astuteness fails . . ." Indeed, there are prescribed rituals of mourning in Judaism that recognize the importance of ordinary grieving. or example, the custom of "sitting shiva." The word "shiva" comes from the Hebrew word *shiv'ah*, which means "seven". "Sitting shiva" refers to the week-long mourning period, after the death of a first-degree relative. At the same time, the Judaic tradition recognizes that mourning and grief must have limits—both for the sake of the mourner and of the community as a whole. "We should not mourn excessively," the Talmud says, "because we must not impose upon the community a hardship that would be difficult to bear." In this respect, the rabbis were not far from the view held by the ancient Stoics; for example, the Roman philosopher and statesman Seneca remarked that "We can be pardoned for having given way to tears, so long as they have not run down in excessive quantities . . ."

Finally, in the Jewish mystical tradition known as *Hasidism,* we find the idea that even in our grief, there may be a transcendent meaning that is concealed from us. Thus, a Hasidic saying states,

"Even in the deepest sinking there is the hidden purpose of an ultimate rising. Thus it is for all; from none is the source of light withheld unless one withdraws from it. Therefore the most important thing is not to despair."

- ### Joyfulness, Gratitude and Pleasure

It is fair to say that, for all its awareness of life's "slings and arrows," Judaism is basically an optimistic and life-affirming faith. The traditional Jewish toast of *"L'chaim!"*—"To life!"—speaks volumes on the Jewish world view. Furthermore, unlike more ascetic and self-denying traditions—and we must include *some* Buddhist and Stoic writers in this camp—Judaism affirms the role of *pleasure* in our lives. The Talmud boldly proclaims, "Every man must render an account before God of all [permissible] good things he beheld and did not enjoy." Furthermore, "Whoever denies himself a little wine is a sinner—and the man who denies himself too many things is a greater sinner." Note, however, the important qualifiers: we are entitled to "permissible" pleasures; the amount of wine permitted is only "a little"; and it is only the one who denies himself "too many" things who is deemed a sinner.

Here we find the brilliant paradox in rabbinical Judaism: pleasure is good, but excessive indulgence undermines the flourishing life. For example, in general, drunkenness is severely condemned in rabbinical Judaism—except on one occasion. On the holiday of Purim—which celebrates the deliverance of the Jews from a plot by the Persian Empire to annihilate them—drunkenness is actually mandated! Referencing, respectively, the villain and the hero of the Purim story, the Talmud instructs us that, on Purim, ". . . one should drink till he cannot tell the difference between "Cursed be Haman" and "Blessed be Mordecai." You may read that as "getting very drunk!"

Nonetheless, by far the predominant strain in Judaism is "moderation in all things", including pleasure. Furthermore, "pleasure" is to be understood not as mere sensual gratification, but as something deeper and more abiding. For example, the Judaic tradition stresses the importance of friends, family, and community as elements of the "flourishing life." The marital bond is a special source of joy, and great importance is accorded to what is called *shalom bayit*—literally, "peace at home". The term really implies something like "domestic harmony," and both man and wife must labor to preserve it. This is such an important value in Judaism that one is even permitted to "alter the truth"—what we would call, "telling a little white lie"—in order to preserve domestic peace. The Talmud tells us that if a man and woman work together, they bring God's presence into their homes—and that is perhaps the greatest joy of all.

Finally, Judaism stresses the importance of *gratitude*—not just as an ethical imperative, but as a prerequisite for genuine "happiness" in the sense we have defined. Thus, a Talmudic saying asks, "Who is rich?" and replies, "He who rejoices in his portion." Similarly, the 13th century Jewish sage, Jacob Anatoli, taught that, "If a person cannot get what he wants, he ought to want what he can get." This is strikingly similar to the Stoic teaching from Seneca: "It is in no man's power to have whatever he wants; but he has it in his power not to wish for what he hasn't got, and cheerfully make the most of the things that do come his way."

Judaism is an incomparably rich and complex religious, ethical, and spiritual tradition, and more of its many layers will be revealed in subsequent chapters. And, as we'll see in the next section, many of Judaism's themes—such as self-restraint, moderation, and gratitude—are also prominent elements of Buddhism.

Buddhism: A Brief History of Its Core Beliefs

Just as Judaism may be seen as a religion, a philosophy, a culture, etc., so, too, Buddhism may be viewed in a variety of ways. Indeed, the enormous range of Buddhist sects, schools, and philosophies rivals or surpasses even the diversity within Judaism. And yet, as we'll see, there are common features in Buddhism that unite these diverse views and communities. It's fair to begin with the Buddha himself—or rather, with a *particular* Buddha, known as "Shakyamuni" (meaning, "the sage of the Shakya tribe"). The name Shakyamuni is attached to the figure of *Siddhartha Gautama*, who is believed to have lived from about 560 BCE to 480 BCE. The term "Buddha" simply means "awakened one," and was applied to Gautama by his followers after he attained "enlightenment" (*bodhi*, in Sanskrit) around the age of 35. But in the *Mahayana* division of Buddhism—more on that shortly—"buddhahood" is not restricted to the single person of Gautama; rather, it is a *transcendent principle* that has infused many "Buddhas" throughout the ages.

Historically, Buddhism arose in India as a reaction to the predominant religion of Hinduism—even though the two faiths share a number of concepts and beliefs. While there are hundreds of Buddhist schools and sects, there are three main divisions of Buddhism: *Theravada*, *Mahayana*, and *Vajrayana* (Tibetan) Buddhism. The chief differences among these divisions are summarized in **Table 1**, in the appendix of this book. Mahayana Buddhism is the largest division of Buddhism, probably accounting for over half the Buddhist population. Mahayana is usually considered more "liberal" and accessible to the average person than the Theravada tradition, which is mainly found in monastic settings. Most Americans are familiar with Zen Buddhism, which is one of many Mahayana schools.

While the theological differences among the Buddhist divisions are of great interest to scholars, they are not critical to our everyday application of Buddhist ideals in pursuit of the "flourishing life." Nevertheless—in order to appreciate the diversity within Buddhism—it's helpful to go over some features that distinguish the three main divisions within Buddhism.

- *Theravada* ("The Way of the Elders") is largely a monastic discipline, and is found mostly in south and southeast Asia, in countries such as Sri Lanka, Thailand, and Cambodia. In the Theravada tradition, the "perfected disciple" is known as an *arhat*—usually a monk who is said to have reached total awakening and achieved *Nirvana*. Nirvana is not a "place," like heaven in the Judeo-Christian tradition; rather, it is a *state of being* that follows the elimination of all craving and anger. You can probably guess that only a select few, following the Theravada path, ever achieve this exalted state.

- In contrast, the Mahayana school emphasizes the concept of the *bodhisattva*, an enlightened and compassionate being who postpones his or her own achievement of nirvana, in order to help others reach their own enlightenment. In Mahayana Buddhism, spiritual liberation (*moksha*) is available to all, not just a few monks. Furthermore, as Prof. Paul Flesher has noted, the Mahayana tradition believes that

    "All human beings participate in the Buddha's nature; that is to say, all humans have the essence of Buddha within themselves. Thus the goal of Mahayana Buddhism is for everyone to realize their true Buddha nature. This goal is the same as

attaining nirvana (the Theravadan goal), but it is
focused on the Buddha and each person's imitation
of the Buddha." (*Exploring Religions* website).

There is an important ethical dimension of Mahayana
Buddhism, embodied in the "The Six Paramitas" or "Six
Perfections." These are usually described as *generosity,
moral discipline, patience, diligence, concentration,*
and *wisdom* (Tulku, 1993), and are essentially the
characteristics of all who aspire to be a *bodhisattva*
(literally, "one seeking enlightenment"). Nevertheless,
Vietnamese Zen master Thich Nhat Hanh suggests that
the Six Perfections are applicable to *all* of us, in our daily
lives. He says, "We are on the shore of suffering, anger,
and depression, and we want to cross over to the shore
of well-being." (The Heart of the Buddha's Teaching,
p. 192). To cross over, we need to practice the Six
Perfections. We'll mention these again when we discuss
the Eightfold Path, in relation to Buddhism in general.

Zen Buddhism represents the fusion of the
Mahayana tradition with the important Chinese
religious tradition, Daoism (or, *Taoism*) While we won't
discuss Daoism in any detail, it's useful to mention a
central teaching of Daoism, called *wu-wei*. The Zen
scholar Alan Watts describes *wu-wei* as "non-straining;"
it is also sometimes described as "effortless action." One
practitioner of Daoism, Elizabeth Reninger, describes
wu-wei as ". . . a state of being in which our actions
are quite effortlessly in alignment with the ebb and flow
of the elemental cycles of the natural world." (http://
taoism.about.com/od/wuwei/a/wuwei.htm)

The core of Daoist belief is the idea of not forcing
or "grasping" one's way through life; but instead, living

life spontaneously, in harmony with the natural order of things (*Dao* or *Tao*). This view is close in spirit to that of the Stoics, and their principle of living in harmony with the "Logos," as we will see. "Wu-wei" also constitutes an important dimension of Zen Buddhism.

Zen Buddhism comprises two main schools. *Soto Zen* emphasizes "sitting meditation" (*zazen*); *Rinzai Zen* emphasizes use of the *koan*, or paradoxical statement—for example, the well-known question, "What is the sound of one hand clapping?" Achieving direct, immediate, non-cognitive insight is a key element of Rinzai Zen, and the most important hoped-for result of contemplating *koan* riddles.

- Tibetan Buddhism (*Vajrayana*) is the smallest of the three divisions and is familiar to many Americans because of the Dalai Lama, the spiritual leader of the Tibetan people. The Dalai Lama is regarded as the incarnation of Chenrezig (referred to as *Avalokiteshvara* in India), the bodhisattva of compassion. Indeed, the Dalai Lama has summarized his faith as precisely one *whose core value is compassion.*

Tibetan Buddhism combines features of both Mahayana and Theravada. Like Mahayana schools, Tibetan Buddhism recognizes many Buddhas and bodhisattvas. But, like Theravada, Tibetan Buddhism is mostly a monastic discipline. Meditation is an important part of Vajrayana, and may be aided by the use of special hand gestures called *mudras* and highly-compressed chants called *mantras.* Tibetan Buddhism also includes elements of *Tantra.* While you might associate this term with esoteric sexual practices, it really refers to the concept of *transmuting desire*, rather than stifling it. As Wallace puts it, Tantra uses "the energy of desire to move us along the [spiritual] path." (p. 188).

Also central to Tibetan Buddhism is the concept of *non-duality*. Teachers like Chagdud Tulku tell us that the sharp division we often make between self and others, between "mine" and "yours," leads to selfishness and aggression. Tibetan Buddhism teaches us that by overcoming such duality, we are able to let go of much resentment and enmity. Finally, the "Six Perfections," discussed as a feature of Mahayana Buddhism, also figure prominently in Tibetan Buddhism.

Common Threads in Buddhism

So, with this brief sketch in mind, what are the main beliefs held in common by most Buddhist schools and divisions? And—more relevant to our exploration of the fulfilled life—what do these beliefs tell us about human existence and happiness?

Central to all Buddhist schools are three universal values, termed "The Three Jewels" (*triratna*): the *Buddha*, the *Dhamma*, and the *Sangha*. The first jewel, the Buddha, seems self-explanatory. However, as Thich Nhat Hanh has observed, reliance on the Buddha also means relying on "the Buddha in myself," consistent with the view that "we ourselves are the Buddha." (The Heart of the Buddha's Teaching, p. 162). The Buddha's teachings are collectively termed the *Dhamma* (in Pali) or the *Dharma* (in Sanskrit). Finally, the *Sangha* is the monastic community of Buddhist monks and nuns, in the narrow sense of the term. However, more broadly, *Sangha* refers to the entire community of spiritual practitioners of Buddhism, including laypersons.

Let's begin with the core Buddhist beliefs known popularly as "The Four Noble Truths"—although, as Prof. Jay Garfield has observed, it would be more accurate to call these "The Four Truths that Contribute to a Noble Life." These four basic principles are sometimes stated as follows:

1. Suffering [*dukha*] is a basic part of life.
2. Suffering is caused by selfish craving [*tanha*].
3. We can eliminate suffering by eliminating selfish craving.
4. Suffering due to selfish craving can be eliminated by following "The Noble Eightfold Way."

These four truths are often stated in different ways; for example, as "Existence is unhappiness; unhappiness is caused by selfish craving . . ." etc. Sometimes the Sanskrit term, *dukha,* is translated as "misery," or "sorrow." The important point is that the Buddha—like a good physician—has provided us with a "diagnosis" for our woes, and a "prescription" for the cure—"The Noble Eightfold Way." We'll say more about this shortly; but first, let's delve a bit into this notion of "suffering" [*dukha*].

First, it's important to note that Buddhism isn't as gloomy as it sounds. It really doesn't teach us that life is *nothing but* suffering. Life also has its great joys, of course. In fact, Buddhism doesn't really argue that suffering [*dukha*] is *inherently* or *necessarily* built into our existence. Yes, there are many causes and occasions for suffering, from financial misfortune to illness and death. But as the scholar E.A. Burtt explains, these unfortunate events

> ". . . would not make us unhappy were it not for the blind demandingness (*tanha*) in our nature, which leads us to ask of the universe . . . more than it is ready or even able to give." (from *The Teachings of the Compassionate Buddha*).

As a psychiatrist and ethicist, if I had to name the number one cause of unhappiness in the average person's life, I would point immediately to *tanha*! Indeed, millions of hours of psychotherapy could probably be averted, if everybody were to embrace one simple (yet profound) truth: *if you ask more of the universe than it can give, you will most certainly be unhappy. If you stop doing that, there is at least a good chance your unhappiness will decrease dramatically.*

But how, after all, do we stop ourselves from falling into the snare of *tanha*? Nobody would claim that this is easy; nor has anybody I have ever met succeeded completely in avoiding *dukha*. Such an individual would justifiably be called an *arhat*, a *bodhisattva*, a "saint," or a "Stoic master!" Nonetheless, Buddhism does provide a route toward the elimination of *tanha*, called the "Eightfold Path." In brief, this consists of a series of steps, including *right understanding; right purpose; right speech; right conduct; right vocation; right effort; right mindfulness* (or alertness); *and right concentration.* These eight components are sometimes grouped into three more encompassing categories, termed *prajna* (wisdom), *sila* (moral conduct) and *samadhi* (concentration).

We'll say more about several of these eight steps in the section on the "four key areas" of Buddhist belief. According to the teachings of the Buddha (called *dharma*), the one who moves progressively through these eight stages achieves *moksha* (liberation) and ultimately enters *Nirvana*—which, as noted earlier, is a state of mind and being, not a "place." Notice that the Eightfold Path is fundamentally *action-oriented*—it's not enough to "think good thoughts." We must also orient our *behavior* in the right direction. So there is a profoundly *ethical* dimension to the Buddhist spiritual path, in which "right conduct" (*sila*) is paramount. As former Buddhist monk Stephen Batchelor argues in his book, *Buddhism Without Beliefs,* "the dharma is not something to believe in, but something to do."

We have already mentioned the "Six Paramitas" (Six Perfections) in connection with Mahayana Buddhism, but now we may ask, "What's the relationship between the Six Perfections and the Eightfold Path?" There is clearly considerable overlap between the two, but the Eightfold Path is applicable to all who seek to eliminate suffering (*dukha*). In partial contrast, the Six Perfections are usually considered the spiritual traits of the *bodhisattva* ("enlightenment being"). Thus, the Six Paramitas are basically a further development of the Eightfold Path.

Finally, there are several doctrines in Buddhism that I would call "metaphysical," such as the concepts of *karma* and *samsara*. Karma means "intentional action." In popular parlance, "karma" is often summed up in the old saying, "What goes around, comes around." More accurately, karma is understood as "the ethical law of cause and effect" that operates in a totally impersonal way. As Prof. Stephen Prothero puts it,

> ". . . according to [*karma*], which, like gravity, operates without divine intervention, positive consequences follow from good actions and negative consequences from bad actions—either in this lifetime or in a future incarnation." (*Religious Literacy*, p. 196)

Another way of putting it: karma means that ". . . the seeds of our actions continue with us from one lifetime to the next and do not get lost." (Chodron, p. 59).

And, it is karma that "drives" *samsara*—the endless cycle of birth, death, and rebirth that Buddhists believe governs all of existence. Since Buddhists deny the existence of an eternal soul, they believe that it is one's "consciousness" that is reborn, and that ". . . you get the rebirth you deserve." (Prothero, Religious Literacy, p. 218). So, for example: a person who does little but harm and abuse others in this life may be reincarnated in some "lower" form of life, such as a snake.

These ideas are certainly important in Buddhism, but they take us into very speculative and non-verifiable realms. As Stephen Batchelor argues, we need not embrace these doctrines in order to pursue the practices, and reap the benefits, of Buddhism. For readers who want to learn more about these ideas, the reference list will provide ample sources of information. However, there are three Buddhist concepts that deserve some discussion—*shunyata*, or "emptiness;" *anatman*, or "non-self"; and *anicca*, or "impermanence." These are complex ideas, but they have an important connection to our aim of achieving the flourishing life—so let's spend a little time trying to understand them.

"Emptiness" in Buddhism has to do with the *absence of independent (or "intrinsic") existence*. What does this mean? The principle of emptiness asserts that *nothing exists in and of itself, apart from other entities, and apart from our own perceptions and conceptions*. Here's a very simple example. You have probably driven on a highway on a very hot summer's day, and seen a kind of rippling effect on the pavement ahead of you that looks like water on the road surface. We call this a "mirage." But when we analyze this experience, we realize that the "mirage" has no independent existence, apart from the hot pavement; the bending of light by a heated layer of air; and the way in which our brain "processes" and interprets the stimuli received by our retinas. Thus, the mirage is "empty" of any inherent or independent existence. (A related concept in Buddhism is termed "interdependent co-arising", and is defined by Thich Nhat Hanh as the principle that ". . . cause and effect co-arise . . . and everything is a result of multiple causes and conditions. The egg is in the chicken, and the chicken is in the egg").

Here is another example of how, in Buddhist philosophy, nothing exists independently. As Connor Wood, MTS, has eloquently observed,

"A boat has no independent existence apart from the materials that were used to craft it; the forest in which the trees grew; the hands of the boatwrights who made it; the food those workers ate; the farmers who grew that food; the soil it grew in; the water on which the boat floats; the plans on which the boat's design was based; the eyes that see the boat in the harbor; [and] the hands that hold its rudder." (personal communication, 8/29/12)

The difficult concept for most of us to grasp is that, in Buddhism, *everything, including our minds, shares this property of "emptiness" or "dependent existence."* Even what we call "the self" is really a construction that depends on the existence of other people—after all, how else do we become aware of our "selves" as separate entities, except in relation to others? The concept of "self" also depends on our own ability to synthesize the endless stream of our memories, sensations, and desires into a seemingly coherent whole. But in Buddhism, the "self" is considered a kind of fiction or illusion—a concept called *anatman* ("non-self").

We need not delve too deeply into these closely-related ideas—*shunyata* and *anatman*—to appreciate that they have important implications for how we see the world; how we behave toward other human beings; and how we live our lives. *Both concepts point us toward the inter-dependence of all things and all creatures.* This leads, in turn, toward an openness to, and compassion toward, our fellow human beings. We are put in mind of those famous lines penned by the poet John Donne:

"No man is an island entire of itself; every man is a piece of the continent, a part of the main . . . any man's death diminishes me, because I am involved

in mankind. And therefore never send to know for
whom the bell tolls; it tolls for thee."

Finally, we have the concept of *anicca*. This is usually translated
as "impermanence" or "uncertainty." The Buddhist master Ajahn
Chah (1918-92) believed that much of our suffering stems from
our unwillingness to accept the *impermanence* of all things. Sure,
we often hear the expressions, "Nothing lasts forever" or "Easy
come, easy go"—but how many of us have really understood the
implications of impermanence? For example: how many of us
ever pause to consider our own mortality? As Ajahn Chah notes,
the Buddha taught us

> ". . . to look in the present and see the impermanence
> of body and mind, of all phenomena as they appear
> and cease, without grasping at any of it. If we can
> do this, we will experience peace. This peace comes
> because of letting go . . ." (from *everything arises,*
> *everything falls away*).

This idea is picked up again in Stoicism, as we'll soon see;
and also has its echoes in rabbinical Judaism. If we really could
accept the idea that everything is impermanent, Buddhism tells
us, we would not be so fiercely attached to ideas, concepts, or
beliefs—or even people. Just imagine how politics in this country
might change, if partisans on all sides could "let go" of their rigid
ideologies. Imagine how the animosity between religious groups
would diminish! And imagine how our everyday unhappiness
might melt away, if we could detach ourselves from our own
preconceptions and prejudices. All this, the Buddhists tell us,
is possible if we can embrace the idea of impermanence. Rabbi
Rami Shapiro has put the idea more colloquially: "Don't take life
so seriously—it's only temporary!"

* * *

Now that we've had our whirlwind tour of Buddhist ideas, let's discuss four key areas of Buddhism bearing on human thought, feeling, and conduct, just as we did for Judaism.

- **Tact, Empathy, and Compassion**

In Mahayana Buddhism, we find a revered figure named Avalokiteshvara, known as "The Bodhisattva of Infinite Compassion." You'll recall that a *bodhisattva* is one who is on the path to enlightenment, but who foregoes complete enlightenment in order first to help all *other* beings attain this state. Among these awakened beings, Avaloketsehvara is especially renowned for compassion (in Sanskrit, *karuna*) and understanding.

Buddhism, we have said, aims toward "awakening." And as Stephen Batchelor has observed, "Compassion is the very heart and soul of awakening." I take him to mean something like this: we are most truly "awake" to being human when we realize that our fate is bound up in that of others, and in the fate of the world. (As we noted above, compassion is linked to *shunyata* and the interdependence of all things).

But what is compassion? The Tibetan Buddhist nun Thubten Chodron defines it as "the wish for all sentient beings to be free from suffering and its causes." (p. 28). However, Prof. Jay Garfield makes an interesting observation regarding *karuna*. He notes that *karuna* is not "an emotion," and is not merely "sloppy sympathy" for somebody who is suffering. It is not enough simply to have warm feelings for the downtrodden, or to have "pie in the sky" schemes for helping these unfortunates. Rather, Prof. Garfield insists, *karuna* implies a concrete *commitment to moral action* that will actually benefit others.

But while *karuna* is not simply an emotion, it is fair to say that true compassion does require *empathy*—indeed, the two words are closely related. The Tibetan Buddhist teacher Chagdud Tulku Rinpoche (1930-2002) asks, "How do we generate compassion? We begin by contemplating the difficulties of others, and then we put ourselves in their shoes." This is empathy. The opposite of empathy and compassion is self-centeredness—which of course is anathema to Buddhism. So perhaps we can say that *karuna* is best understood as *empathic appreciation of another's suffering combined with a realistic commitment to do something about it.*

In Buddhist teaching, compassion extends not only to other creatures, but to the world itself. As the Vietnamese monk Thich Nhat Hanh has observed,

> "Aware of the suffering caused by exploitation, social injustice, stealing and oppression, I vow to cultivate loving-kindness and learn ways to work for the well-being of people, animals, plants, and minerals."
> (p. 93, Living Buddha, Living Christ).

Note how Thich Nhat Hanh combines both the *inner state* of "loving-kindness" with the commitment to *working* for the well-being of others.

But how do we cultivate such high-minded feelings for those individuals we really dislike—and, perhaps, who dislike us? There is a renowned teaching in Buddhism that instructs us to see every human being as if he or she were *our mother*! The exercise is designed to increase our compassion for that person, even if we regard him as an enemy. (As Prof. Stephen Prothero has noted, this exercise may not work well if you have very strong negative feelings toward your mother!). We find a similar teaching in the mystical strain of Judaism that grew up around Rabbi Moses Cordovero (1522-1570), who urged us to picture everyone around us an innocent, newborn baby. The ancient Stoics, too, stressed the need for compassion. The Roman emperor and Stoic philosopher Marcus Aurelius (121-180 CE) put it this way: "A man's joy is to do what is proper to man; and man's proper work is kindness to his fellow man."

As we'll see, you can leave out a good deal of fancy theology and metaphysics, and still do very well as a Jew, a Buddhist, or a Stoic by living a life of compassion, tempered by reason!

• Anger, Rage, and Revenge

Buddhism understands anger (*vyapada*) as the result of our natural human tendency to "identify" with external events and their associated emotions. For example, somebody cuts you off in traffic, and you feel your heart pounding and your head throbbing. If someone were to ask you how you feel at that moment, you would probably say, "I *am* angry!" By using the verb "to be" to link "I" with "angry", you are basically saying that *you and the anger are one.* The Buddhist teacher B. Alan Wallace suggests that if you "attend" to the anger rather than identifying with it, the anger will dissipate. That is, you can say to yourself, "Aha, the event of anger has arisen again!" This separation of you from the anger and the inciting event gives you a bit of "breathing room." This requires you to exercise "mindfulness"—and you may recall that the seventh stage on the Eightfold Path is called, "Right Mindfulness." Anger arises when we fail to exercise right mindfulness. But when we make use of this faculty, we find ourselves suddenly "freed up." For example, you can choose whether to ignore the obnoxious driver; chase him down; take down his license number; or put on the radio to distract yourself. Furthermore, as Wallace points out, for anger to persist, it needs to be "fed." You might, for example, keep your anger alive by imagining all the nasty things you'd love to do to avenge yourself against that guy who cut you off! Or, you can choose to stop focusing on those revenge fantasies, and shift your attention to something else.

There is a wonderful mental exercise that the Buddha prescribes, for times when we feel overcome by anger. As paraphrased from Thich Nhat Hanh, the exercise has five stages:

1.   Recognition: Saying to yourself, "I know that anger is in me."
2.   Acceptance: You "own" your anger and do not deny it.
3.   Embracing: You imagine that you are cradling your anger in your arms, the way a mother cradles a baby.
4.   Looking deeply: You try to understand what brought about your anger.
5.   Insight: You begin to see that there were many causes and conditions for your anger, and many reasons why the "baby" is crying out.

This exercise may seem like an elaborate variation on the old saw, "Count to ten when you're angry!" But it clearly goes much deeper—it is a way of realizing that when we become angry, we are failing to understand that its root causes *are within us*. Anger arises because we are not exercising "right mindfulness." Similarly, Buddhism sees *vengeance* as another failure to realize right mindfulness. As Thich Nhat Hanh observes with respect to capital punishment,

> "The death penalty is a sign of weakness . . . killing a person does not help him or us. We have to look collectively to find ways we can really help. Our enemy is not the other person . . . if we look deeply into ourselves, we can see that their act was a manifestation

of our collective consciousness. We are all filled with
violence, hatred and fear, so why blame someone
whose upbringing was without love or understanding?"
(Living Buddha, Living Christ, p.76).

We may not necessarily agree with this view—after all, was
the act of an assassin really a manifestation of our collective
consciousness?—but it is characteristic of much Buddhist
thinking.

• **Worry, Sorrow, and Depression**

If, as the Four Noble Truths tell us, "Life is suffering;" and if
everything is "impermanent" as Buddhism teaches—then surely
Buddhists believe it is perfectly normal to walk around feeling
sorrowful, worried, and depressed, right? Well, no—not at all!
As Chagdud Tulku teaches us, "It's true that we can't really grasp
and hold onto things, but we can use that knowledge to look at
life differently, as a very brief and precious opportunity." (p.32).
Similarly, Thich Nhat Hanh tells us that ". . . Every time you
take one mindful step, you have a chance to go from the land of
sorrow to the land of joy." (*Heart*, p. 192).

What is required is neither a pessimistic nor an
overly-optimistic view of life's "slings and arrows"—what we have
called *dukha*—but a realistic outlook. Writer John Snelling has
put it this way: "When we face up to the dark side of life . . . we
begin to appreciate the full grandeur and challenge of human
existence . . . [then] we can start to do something about changing
our lives, putting them on a deeper, more authentic footing."
[*Handbook*, p. 44].

• Joyfulness, Gratitude and Pleasure

Buddhism draws us toward more than just a release from suffering: it also teaches us that there is *great joy* to be found in life—if only we develop the right attitude or "mindfulness." Chagdud Tulku reminds us that we must find joy as soon as we arise: "Rejoice that you didn't die in the night, knowing that you have one more useful day . . . meet the day with an altruistic intention to help others." (p. 36).

Gratitude is, indeed, central to the spirit of Buddhism. As a famous Buddhist saying puts it,

> "Let us rise up and be thankful, for if we didn't learn
> a lot today, at least we learned a little, and if we didn't
> learn a little, at least we didn't get sick, and if we got
> sick, at least we didn't die; so, let us be thankful."

The issue of "pleasure" is a bit complicated in Buddhism. As we saw in the Judaic tradition, pleasure as such is fine, so long as we are not unduly attached to it or controlled by it. One of the very oldest Buddhist Scriptures, the *Sutta Nipata*, admirably summarizes this "moderate" Buddhist attitude toward pleasure:

> "All the delightful things of the world—sweet
> sounds, lovely forms, all the pleasant tastes and
> touches and thoughts—these are all agreed to bring
> happiness if they are not grasped and possessed.
> But if you regard them merely as pleasures for your
> own use and satisfaction and do not see them as
> passing wonders, they will bring suffering." [from
> *The Buddha Speaks: A Book of Guidance from the
> Buddhist Scriptures*, by Anne Bancroft]

This same text warns us against "the rivers of craving," which can overwhelm us in our own frantic pursuit of pleasure. With this, the Rabbis of the Talmud would have agreed!

Stoicism: A Brief History of its Core Beliefs

Stoicism as a formal school dates to roughly the third century BCE, when Zeno of Citium (333-261 BCE) began teaching in Athens. The Stoics got their name from an Athenian building called the "Stoa Poikile" ("Painted Porch"), where Zeno used to lecture. Other well-known Stoic philosophers include Zeno's pupil, Cleanthes (331-232 BCE); the Roman statesman, Seneca (4 BCE-65 CE); the former slave, Epictetus (ca. 55-135 CE); and our good friend the Roman emperor, Marcus Aurelius (121-180 CE).

Now, for many of us raised in the 60s—with its "Let it all hang out!" credo—the idea of being "stoical" sounds a lot like being, well, uptight and stuffy. Many "boomers" who came of age in the Woodstock era were steeped in the idea that *expressing* emotion is more important than understanding or modulating it. For the most part, the culture of the 1960s did not emphasize how our emotional over-reactions can detract from our happiness. In contrast, the pioneers of cognitive-behavioral therapy (CBT), such as Dr. Albert Ellis and Dr. Aaron Beck, have long recognized this fact, and Ellis often alluded to the views of Epictetus.

But genuine Stoicism is not about keeping a "stiff upper lip" or tamping down your feelings with an iron rod. On the contrary, Stoicism is a mental and spiritual outlook and discipline that emphasizes *living in harmony with reason, and with Nature's laws*—an idea also found in Taoism and Buddhism. Although you'll find many passages by Stoic writers to support the idea of emotional *modulation*, the Stoic ideal was not an emotionless, unfeeling human being. Rather, the Stoics argued that there is a "moderate middle ground" that best suits us as rational creatures.

The Stoics aimed for what they called *apatheia*—but it would be a mistake to translate this as "apathy" in the negative sense we attach to it today. Rather, *apatheia—literally, "without suffering"*—implies a kind of *equanimity of spirit*, and living life without illusions or pretensions. As Marcus Aurelius tells us, "Perfection of character possesses this: to live each day as if [it were] the last; to be neither feverish nor apathetic; and not to act a part." (Farquharson, 52). The Stoics did not teach us to suppress joy. Rather, they taught us to obtain joy through *virtuous action, in accordance with reason*. The Stoic sage aims to understand "the way things are," and to live accordingly. And, while you don't have to believe in God to be a Stoic, you do need to understand how the universe is, well, *set up*. When we understand and accept the way things are, we find ourselves at peace, and we are free to pursue our higher pleasures. When we refuse to accept the way things are, we make ourselves (and often others) unhappy. For example, if you want friends and family to live forever, you will inevitably be left broken-hearted—you are asking more of the universe than it can possibly deliver, as we saw in the Buddhist concept of *tanha*. In contrast, when you live your life according to Stoic principles, you don't need to tamp down your feelings—rather, the feelings you actually have are *appropriate* to "the way things are."

Similarly, the Stoics did not advocate rooting out all our desires; rather, we are instructed to choose our desires wisely and realistically. When we focus our desires on things we can't control—such as achieving fame and fortune—we set ourselves up for anxiety and disappointment. We find a similar sentiment expressed by the Jewish sage, Rav Eliyahu of Vilna, known as the Vilna Gaon (1720-97). He tells us, "Desires must be purified and idealized, not exterminated" (Baron, 1985).

By now, you may already be thinking, "But aren't there times when we should *not* accept 'the way things are?' When there are terrible social injustices, for example, aren't we obligated to *change* the status quo?" Like Thich Nhat Hanh and other socially "activist" Buddhists, the Stoics would answer with a very clear and forceful "*Yes!*" To understand this, we need to realize that a part of "the way things are" is *our own set of values and aspirations.* Our intention to make the world a better place is no less a part of reality than rocks, trees, or turtles. Our social values are no less real than the social evils we seek to overturn. Thus, we have every right—and even a responsibility—to try to change things for the better. But when we have exerted every effort in doing so, and failed, the Stoics tell us that we are not obligated to make ourselves miserable!

In short, Stoic philosophy may be summed up in that well-known maxim associated with 12-step programs, but originating with the theologian Reinhold Niebuhr (1892-1971): "God grant me the serenity to accept the things I cannot change, courage to change the things I can, and the wisdom to know the difference." Stoicism is not passive acceptance of the status quo. It is a reasoned understanding of the way things are, and a rational determination to improve what can be improved—including ourselves.

* * *

Before examining the four key areas of Stoicism, we can summarize its core beliefs in terms of ten main principles:

- **"*Things do not touch the soul,*"** as Marcus Aurelius put it. Rather, we are perturbed by "the opinion which is within [us]". This is very much in the spirit of Buddhism, as we find in the *Dhammapada*: "We are what we think.

All that we are arises with our thoughts." Shakespeare said much the same thing in *Hamlet*: "There is nothing either good or bad but thinking makes it so."

- *We must always be conscious of our own mortality*. As Marcus bluntly puts it, "Since it is possible that you may depart from life this very moment, regulate every act and thought accordingly." We have already seen how this same concept enters into Judaism and Buddhism.

- *Doing the right thing is really the only thing that matters*, and it lies at the very core of our self-respect. As Marcus puts it, "Never value anything as profitable to yourself which shall compel you to break your promise, to lose your self-respect, to hate anyone, to suspect, to curse [or] to act the hypocrite."

- *Adversity befalls all of us, and we must be prepared to deal with it courageously and forthrightly*. We may also find that misfortune is a good teacher, if only we are open to receiving its lessons. As Shakespeare wrote in *As You Like It*, "Sweet are the uses of adversity."

- *We should be realistic in assessing our own vices and virtues, and not demand perfection of either ourselves or others*. We should not be overly-tolerant of our own failings, but neither should we castigate ourselves when we don't achieve all that we had hoped. Seneca tells us, "What progress . . . have I made? I have begun to be a friend to myself."

- *We need to accept the universe for what it is, and live in harmony with it*, without railing against our "fate" or bemoaning "what might have been." Marcus Aurelius writes that nothing ever happens to us that ". . . is not conformable to the nature of the universe," however perverse or unfair it may seem. The Stoic view is similar to that of the 8th century Buddhist sage and bodhisattva Shantideva, who said, "Why be unhappy about something if it can be fixed? If it cannot be fixed, what does being unhappy help?"

- **We need to live in the "here-and-now."** As Marcus says, "Leave the past to itself, entrust the future to providence, and content yourself with bringing holiness and justice to the present." This is quite similar to the Buddhist teaching, "Do not pursue the past. Do not lose yourself in the future . . . [look] deeply at life as it is, in the very here and now . . ." (from the *Bhaddekaratta Sutta*).

- **We should not be overly affected by the opinions of others,** particularly as regards our own sense of self-worth and moral obligation. Thus, Marcus asks, "Will any man despise me? Let him see to it. But I will see to it that I may not be found doing or saying anything that deserves to be despised." As Keith Seddon puts it in his discussion of Epictetus, those who adhere to Stoicism ". . . must hold to and persist in what they know is best, no matter how cruelly they may be jeered." (Handbook, p. 95).

- **We are all united in the common bond of being.** The Stoics believed that ". . . all things are woven together, and the common bond is sacred" (Marcus Aurelius). Therefore, we must scrupulously avoid senseless hatred and ill will toward our fellow human beings. Indeed, we must cultivate compassion and empathy for all.

- ***We must remain true to our inner nature, and must keep our character pure.*** The Stoics believed that we must always be aware of our innermost values and beliefs, and not be constantly sounding out others as a guide to our lives. Marcus admonishes us to "abide with the Divinity that is within"—a concept that has affinities with the "Buddha nature" that resides within each of us.

Four key areas of Stoic Beliefs

- **Tact, Empathy and Compassion**

The Stoics are usually associated with logic, rationality, and emotional restraint. And yet, as mentioned above, the Stoics had a deeply spiritual view of humanity, based on the premise that all human beings share an unbreakable "common bond." Thus, Marcus Aurelius urges us to

> ". . . consider the connection of all things in the universe and their relation to one another. For in a manner all things are implicated with one another, and all in this way are friendly to one another" (*Meditations*, Book VI).

Marcus reminds us that ". . . men exist for the sake of one another. Teach them then, or bear with them" (Meditations, Book VIII). He also urges us to "connect" empathically with one another: "Enter into every man's ruling faculty; and also let every other man enter into thine" (*Meditations*, Book VIII).

Indeed, for the Stoics, the common bond of our humanity imposes an obligation that goes beyond being tolerant and empathic. We must also cultivate *love* for our fellow human beings. No philosopher has expressed this better than Seneca, who writes:

> "Hatred is not only a vice, but a vice which goes point-blank against Nature. Hatred divides instead of joining and frustrates God's will in human society. One man is born to help another. Hatred makes us destroy one another. Love unites—hatred separates. Love is beneficial—hatred is destructive. Love succors even strangers; hatred destroys the most intimate friendship. Love fills all hearts with joy, hatred ruins all those who possess it. Nature is bountiful, hatred is pernicious. It is not hatred, but mutual love, that holds all mankind together." (from Davis, *Greek and Roman Stoicism*)

• Anger, Rage, and Revenge

The Stoics—like the Rabbis of the Talmud and the sages of Buddhism—took a very dim view of anger and vengeance. In his essay, "On Anger," Seneca describes this emotion as "brief insanity" and adds that "No plague has cost the human race more." (Irvine, p. 159). This doesn't mean that we should be indifferent to injustice or cruelty. On the contrary, we need to take appropriate action to punish wrongdoers and to protect the innocent. But when we really "lose it" and allow ourselves to be overcome by rage, we often undermine these very goals.

The Stoics had several "remedies" for anger and the wish for revenge. Marcus advises that

> "When you run [up] against someone's wrong behavior, go on at once to reflect what similar wrong act of your own there is . . . for if you attend

to this, you will quickly forget your anger . . ."
(*Meditations,* Book X).

In his own understanding of vengeance, Epictetus introduces an important and subtle doctrine of Stoicism; namely, that the one who wrongs us harms *himself* more deeply, and that this renders vengeance unnecessary:

> "He who has erred, or injured another, has indeed no pain in his head; nor loses an eye . . . But, he has injured something greater—his Will, his Reason, the Divine Being within him. He has inflicted upon himself indelible harm which will add to his unhappiness and increase his misfortunes."
> (Bonforte, *The Philosophy of Epictetus*, p. 86).

In this last statement, perhaps we see hints of the Buddhist concept of "karma"—that is, the principle of causality that says, in essence, "What we put out into the world comes back to us" (Wallace, *Tibetan Buddhism*, p. 63)—if not in this life, then (according to Buddhism) in the next!

• Worry, Sorrow, and Depression

Here, the Stoics really come into their own, and their views have become a critical part of modern-day cognitive-behavioral therapies. Like cognitive therapists—and like the Buddhist sages—the Stoics believed that external events do not cause worry, sorrow, and depression. Marcus Aurelius tells us that "Things themselves touch not the soul . . . nor can they turn or move the soul: but the soul turns and moves itself alone . . ." That is, it is our *attitude* toward "things" and events that determines our emotional response. We make ourselves unhappy by holding certain irrational views or persisting in certain self-defeating behaviors. As Prof. William Irvine puts it in his book, *A Guide to the Good Life*, ". . . what is really foolish is to spend your life in a state of self-induced dissatisfaction when satisfaction lies within your grasp, if only you will change your mental outlook" (p. 78).

The Stoics teach us that when "bad stuff" happens, we need not be made miserable by the unfortunate events. Thus, Epictetus says, "Lameness is an impediment to the leg, but not to the Will. Say this to yourself with regard to everything that happens." (Bonforte, p. 68). Indeed, for the Stoics, the Will is really the only thing under our control (assuming we are not suffering from, say, a dementing illness). Epictetus writes, "Within our power are the Will, and all voluntary actions; out of our power are the body and its parts; property, relatives, country, and in short, all our fellow-beings." It is when we put our energy into trying to control these externals, rather than changing our mental state or attitude, that we become upset, dissatisfied, depressed, etc.

Even the great misfortune of illness and pain need not lay us low, the Stoics insist. Thus, Seneca advises the sufferer to ". . . turn your mind to other thoughts and [in] that way, get away from your suffering . . . it is your body, not your mind as well, that is in the grip of ill health . . . even if one cannot always beat it, one can always bear an illness." (Letter LXXVIII).

• Joyfulness, Gratitude and Pleasure

The Stoics did not believe that life ought to be drained of all emotion—only that we need to examine our *negative* emotions and change the irrational attitudes that usually underlie them. In fact, the Stoics were all in favor of living life happily and joyfully, within certain reasonable limits. How to do this? William Irvine points to the Stoic's ability to find satisfaction in the hundreds of small blessings that we all enjoy every day, but which we habitually take for granted. Not only does the Stoic delight in the proverbial glass being "half full," he or she also contemplates the fact that the glass easily could have been broken or stolen! Indeed, carrying this line of reasoning further, the Stoic might also think, "I'm lucky just to be here, alive and well, enjoying this drink." In this regard, a Jewish proverb comes to mind that says much the same thing: "When a Jew breaks his leg, he thanks God he did not break both legs. If he breaks both legs, he thanks God he did not break his neck!"

And, just as the Stoics did not see misery as arising from external events, so, too, they see joy as arising from within. Marcus Aurelius tells us, for example, that

> "Men seek retreats for themselves, houses in the country, sea shores, and mountains . . . But this is altogether a mark of the most common sort of men; for it is in your power whenever you shall choose to retire into yourself. For nowhere either with more quiet or more freedom from trouble does a man retire than into his own soul . . . I affirm that tranquility is nothing else than the good ordering of the mind." (*Meditations*, Book IV).

Arguably, this last statement is a reasonably good synopsis of the entire corpus of Stoic writing!

Summing Up: The Common Features of "JuBuSto"

Having completed our whirlwind tour of three extensive religious and spiritual "territories," can we summarize the main points and claims these traditions have in common? Allowing for differences in vocabulary and emphasis—and for the many variations within each faith—I would point to the following eight principles:

1. It is important to think clearly and carefully about our everyday experience and how we choose to respond to it.

2. There is a direct connection between how much we suffer or flourish in life, and how clearly we think.*

3. There is a realm of human concern outside the narrow interests of "self," and a common bond that unites all human beings.

4. This common bond imposes ethical obligations upon us, and by fulfilling these, we also live a fulfilled life.

5. Limiting our desires and attachments is essential to living the good life.

6. Appreciating impermanence and mortality allows us to find real meaning in life.

7. Being grateful for what we have is essential to the fulfilled and flourishing life.

8. Self-mastery and the avoidance of anger or aggression are essential to the fulfilled and flourishing life.

These common factors will now serve as the nuclei for the remaining chapters in this book.

———————

*As we noted earlier, Zen Buddhism emphasizes *non-cognitive* approaches to insight, and tends to diminish the role of "logic" or linear reasoning as such.

Chapter 2

THINKING CLEARLY
AND AWAKENING TO LIFE

Judaism

"Great is understanding, for it was placed [in a verse] between two Divine Names . . . any person who lacks understanding eventually goes into exile . . ."
—Rabbi Elazar, Talmud (Sanhedrin 89)

"If you have knowledge you have everything."
—Talmud, Nedarim 40b

"One who acts with reason can grasp the proper reverence for the Creator and will act with true piety . . . do not be drawn excessively after emotions."
—Rabbi Judah Lowe ben Bezalel (1520-1609)

"It is the duty of man to subordinate all the faculties of his soul to his reason."
—Maimonides (*Eight Chapters*, 5)

*   *   *

Buddhism

"When confusion is penetrated with understanding, what remains is peace."

—Ajahn Chah

"If one does not protect one's mind, it is not possible to protect one's practice."

—Shantideva

"We are what we think . . . with our thoughts we make the world."

—from the *Dhammapada*

*   *   *

Stoicism

"Because of our neglect to study the proper valuation of the phenomena of existence, we always exaggerate, and represent things to ourselves greater than the reality."

—Epictetus (Discourses, XIX)

"It is in our power to have no opinion about a thing, and not to be disturbed in our soul; for things in themselves have no natural power to form our judgments."

—Marcus Aurelius (Meditations, Book VI)

"Every nature is contented with itself when it goes on its way well; and a rational nature goes on its way

well when in its thoughts it assents to nothing false
or uncertain . . ."

            —Marcus Aurelius (Meditations BookVIII)

Vignette: Marcie's Misunderstanding

Marcie was a 26-year-old, single female who lived with Bob,
her boyfriend of two years. She came into psychotherapy with
a very vague complaint: "I feel like I'm walking through life in a
daze. Or maybe, in a haze. It's like, I bounce from one feeling to
another, like I'm a ping-pong ball." Marcie had been brought up
in a caring but somewhat chaotic household, with three sisters
and two brothers. "We all sort of competed for mom and dad's
attention, like little sparrows. You had to get mom or dad to notice
you, and kind of be on your side, or you'd get out-maneuvered by
big sister or big brother. And, there was never really enough to go
around in our house—not enough food, not enough love! If you
got on mom or dad's bad side, you'd get smacked down pretty
quick—not physically, but with a dirty look, or a snide remark."

Prior to her current relationship with Bob, Marcie had been
in a series of very unsatisfying relationships with men. "I was
kind of a door mat," she told her therapist. "It was like, I'd take
a lot of crap from the guys I'd go out with, just to hang on to
them." Marcie found herself drinking quite heavily throughout
her teens and twenties, "mainly, I think, to numb the pain,
or just get through the week." She earned a modest living as a
computer programmer, but often spent her small paycheck on
luxury items she really didn't need. Often, this involved frequent
shopping sprees that temporarily boosted her mood, but depleted
her finances. "It's like, I want to store up as much stuff as I can,
like a little squirrel stuffing nuts into his cheeks for the winter. I'll

buy all kinds of jewelry, expensive dresses—I'll get a temporary lift, but after a day or two, I just crash."

Marcie described her relationship with Bob as "Basically OK, I guess," and added, "I mean, Bob has never hit me or anything. But when he gets annoyed, he can be pretty sarcastic. I just sort of sit there and take it . . . I guess I should push back, but I'm just afraid of losing him. I just wish Bob would take the time to ask how I'm feeling, and show me a little affection now and then. You know, a little more TLC. I guess I kind of resent Bob, but I put up with him, and he puts up with me. I guess he's kind of my security blanket."

Marcie denied any major mood swings, and had never had prior contact with the mental health system. But now, she described feeling like "a leaf being blown around in the wind." She noted, "People just get on my nerves. Every little thing they do really annoys me. Like, if somebody gives me a dirty look, or acts like they're better than I am, it just drives me around the bend! I mean, nobody has a right to do that! I can get really angry and sometimes, I lose it and just curse them out." Marcie admitted that she occasionally drinks or smokes marijuana "just to get by and get through", though she usually drank or smoked alone. "Bob would probably kill me if he knew," she added. Marcie described herself as feeling "more and more isolated, like I'm just focused on my own needs." Recently, Marcie had started posting provocative video recordings of herself on Youtube, ". . . hoping maybe somebody will hire me for a show or a movie."

Marcie expressed no particular religious or spiritual inclinations, stating, "I wish I could believe all that God stuff, but I really don't. I guess I don't have that spiritual "center" I hear people talking about all the time. To me, this life is it. No heaven, no hell, no pie in the sky when you die! I just try not to think much about old age or dying. It's really kind of a bummer, but I guess that's where we all end up."

Marcie, from the Jewish Perspective

From the rabbinical and Judaic point of view, Marcie is truly a woman "in exile", owing to her lack of "understanding"—but it is a psychological and spiritual exile, brought on by Marcie's self-defeating way of viewing herself and others. Perhaps a saying from the Talmud will illuminate the nature of Marcie's character, as well as shed some light on her habitual ways of thinking. "A person's character may be recognized," the Talmud tells us, "by three things: one's cup, one's purse, and one's anger."* The idea here is that we can tell a great deal about people by observing how they behave when they consume alcohol; how they save and spend money; and how they control (or fail to control) their temper. Alas, Marcie is clearly having problems in all these area, as shown by her excessive alcohol and marijuana use; her profligate spending on luxury items; and her outbursts of anger, in which she "curses out" people who are irritating her. It's fair to say that Marcie is "drawn excessively after emotions", and feels unable to take control of her own moods—or her own life. She feels like "a leaf being blown around in the wind."

There is a larger sense, though, in which Marcie is "in exile." Rabbi Yosef Tropper teaches us that a person's life may be divided into three "relationships": the person's *relationship with himself or herself; her relationship with others; and her relationship with God.* The Jewish tradition teaches that each of us either "keeps faith", or fails to keep faith, in these three ways. (Some Jews might substitute "the Creator" or "the Eternal Mystery" for "God", and some secular Jews would not recognize this third "relationship" at all). Marcie is alienated from her "true self", in that she won't allow herself to deal with the emotional pain in her life. Instead, she drinks and drugs in order to "numb the pain", as she admits. Her "cup" is her coping device, and it distances Marcie from dealing with all that is missing in her life. Furthermore, Marcie is betraying her own body by exposing it to repeated bouts of drinking and drugging. In the Judaic tradition, this is a violation of a principle called *shemirat haguf*—roughly, "taking care of the body."

In the interpersonal sphere, Marcie's relationships are marred by her deep-seated need for *approval* and *security*. Thus, she has acted the part of "doormat" in her relationships with men, and remains unassertive with her boyfriend, out of the fear that Bob will leave her. This probably explains her willingness to put up with Bob's sarcastic attacks and lack of sensitivity. In one of the great teachings of the Talmud, Hillel the Elder asks, "*If I am not for myself, who will be for me?*" (Pirke Avot 1:14). Marcie hasn't found the inner strength or understanding to be her own advocate and—perhaps as a consequence—she is not treated well by others. This is certainly not to "blame" Marcie for the bad behavior of the men in her life—it is simply to acknowledge that when we fail to be advocates "for ourselves", others sense this and will often take advantage of us. As Rabbi Joseph Telushkin comments in his book on Hillel, ". . . if a person is not concerned with his own needs and well-being, why should he expect others to be?" (p. 164).

Marcie has settled for a relationship in which she "puts up" with Bob, and in which Bob puts up with her. Bob rarely takes the time to inquire about Marcie's well-being, and is sometimes quite obnoxious to her. This is certainly not what the rabbis had in mind when they described *shalom bayit*—literally, the "peace of the home" or "domestic peace." *Shalom bayit* implies a loving and respectful relationship between two individuals—in traditional Jewish teaching, as you might expect, between man and wife. Furthermore, the Talmud tells us that

> "*Any love which is dependent on something, when the 'something' ceases, the love ceases. Any love which is not dependent on anything will never cease.*"
> (Pirke Avot, 5:19)

A love that is "dependent on something" is one that relies on the other person for some kind of "supplies" or "goodies"—whether monetary, physical, or emotional. This is really not "love" in any meaningful sense; rather, it is a kind of *symbiosis,* of the sort we find in the animal kingdom. Unfortunately, Marcie seems to have this kind of dependent-symbiotic relationship with Bob, but is not sufficiently aware of this to change it. (Note that she initially describes her relationship with Bob as "Basically OK"—suggesting more than a little "denial" on Marcie's part).

The second part of Hillel's famous question (Pirke Avot 1:14) asks, *"If I am for myself only, what am I?"* Now, you might expect that the question would be *"Who* am I?" But as Rabbi Joseph Telushkin observes in his book on Hillel (citing Professor Louis Kaplan): "If you are only for yourself, you cease to be a real human being, and you become no longer a 'who' but a 'what'." (p. 165). Unfortunately for Marcie, her life seems to be taking that turn. She describes feeling, "more and more isolated, like I'm just focused on my own needs." In the Jewish tradition, as Rabbi Telushkin points out, ". . . it is wrong to ignore the broader community of which we are also a part." Indeed, this is a direct consequence of the Judaic view that everyone is created "in God's image and therefore worthy of . . . [our] help." (Telushkin, p. 167).

As for Marcie's provocative video recordings, we are reminded of Hillel's teaching (Pirke Avot 1:13) that, "One who seeks a name loses one's name" and of the Talmudic teaching, "From him who seeks greatness, greatness flees; but him who flees from greatness, greatness follows." *(Erubin* 13b). Finally, Marcie says that she does not believe in God—and that's certainly her perfect right. But by becoming primarily focused on her own needs, she has also removed herself from the emotional and spiritual connectedness we are meant to feel with our fellow human beings. Thus, the Talmud tells us, "Do not separate yourself from the community . . ." (Pirke Avot 4:7).

Now if you recall the title of this chapter—"Thinking Clearly and Awakening to Life"—you might be wondering what Marcie's predicament has to do with "thinking clearly", or with "understanding." After all, aren't Marcie's problems really rooted in her character and upbringing? Certainly, psychologists and psychiatrists could easily point to many factors in Marcie's childhood that would explain some of her present attitudes and behaviors—I'll say more on this in the section on "Synthesis."

But in the Jewish tradition, there is a direct connection between *rational thinking*—or "understanding"—and one's character. The most famous proponent of this view was the great medieval philosopher and physician, Moses ben Maimon (called Maimonides; ca. 1135-1204). As the epigram at the beginning of this chapter indicates, Maimonides believed that, "It is the duty of man to subordinate all the faculties of his soul to his reason." Furthermore, in his treatise entitled, "Laws Concerning Character Traits," Maimonides suggests that our character is in fact inseparable from our *degree of rational understanding*. In fact, in Hebrew, the title of his treatise is *Hilkhot De'ot*. The second word, *De'ot*, is the plural of *de'ah*, which may be translated as "knowledge" or "intellect." Sometimes *Hilkhot De'ot* is translated as, "Laws of Knowledge." In essence, Maimonides uses the term "de'ah" to refer to a *state of mind* or an attitude (Weiss & Butterworth, p. 27). So, for example, in discussing vengeance, Maimonides points out that "according to those who *understand*," nothing is worth taking vengeance. He refers over and over to "the wise person" or "disciples of the wise" in describing the nature of a good character. Thus, for Maimonides, *it is our "rational faculty" that allows us to tell the difference between proper and improper actions*—no rational faculty, no proper behavior! It is also our ability to think clearly that allows us to remain unperturbed in the face of life's "slings and arrows." Thus, Maimonides tells us, "The more mental training [one] has, the less affected [one] will be by luck or misfortune." *(Rules of Health)*. We'll explore this theme in detail, in chapter 3.

In Marcie's case, Maimonides would likely attribute her feeling like "a leaf being blown around in the wind" to her lack of clear, rational thinking—in effect, to her faulty knowledge of the world and others. A "Maimonidean" analysis of Marcie's problem might go something like this:

> "Marcie has a distorted understanding of the world, herself, and others. She thinks she can "get through" life by refusing to deal with her problems and by "numbing" herself with alcohol and marijuana; but this is irrational and self-defeating. Marcie also fails to realize that our bodies are sacred gifts, and that we have a responsibility to take good care of them. Furthermore, Marcie believes that the acquisition of material goods will somehow bring her happiness, even though she admits that a few days after her buying sprees, her mood plummets again. She believes it's better to put up with abuse than to assert one's own needs and interests, because she is afraid of being on her own—and erroneously believes she must rely on another to support her emotionally. She believes that her moods are controlled and driven by others, and doesn't understand that it is her subjective *reaction* to these others that drives her "around the bend." She believes that by indulging in fits of anger, she will somehow modify the behavior of those who offend her; but this is truly misguided thinking! Finally, Marcie believes that it's best to avoid thinking about old age or dying; but in fact, it's by contemplating these realities that we are able to re-evaluate what's really important in our lives."

This last point regarding death is sometimes put in a more optimistic way, in the Jewish tradition. For example, Rabbi Joseph Gelberman would begin classes and services by saying that when he woke up in the morning and felt pain in his legs, he would praise the Lord. When asked why, he replied, "If I didn't feel pain, I would be dead and feel nothing! The Lord has let me live for another day and I'm alive! Praise the Lord!" (from Beliefnet).

Finally, there is a sense in which Marcie has yet to achieve what the Buddhists call the "awakened" life, and what Rabbi Rabbi Dovid Rosenfeld calls living with "awareness":

> "When the Torah instructs us to choose life, the meaning is not simply that we behave. It means that we be alive—that we live with awareness. We must understand the gravity of life and recognize the significance of our actions. And however we decide to live, it must be a conscious decision." (mlife-owner@ torah.org; on behalf of; dar@torah.org)

*I have taken several liberties with the actual wording, which is as follows: R. Ila'I said: There are three things by which you can tell whether a person has a decent character: by his cup [if his mind is at ease after he drank wine], by his purse [by the way he deals in money matters] and by his anger [if he controls his temper]. Some say: by his laughter too. [Eruvin 65b; translated by A.Y. Finkel, *Ein Yaakov*].

The Buddhist Perspective

You will recall from Chapter 1 that Buddhism is based on the "Four Noble Truths", the first of which states that "Life is characterized by suffering" (*dukha*). But you may also recall that suffering is not seen as *inherently* or *necessarily* built into our existence. To remind us of what E.A. Burtt observed: the unpleasant events and people in our lives

> ". . . would not make us unhappy were it not for the blind demandingness (*tanha*) in our nature, which leads us to ask of the universe . . . more than it is ready or even able to give." (from *The Teachings of the Compassionate Buddha*).

Looking at Marcie's sad experiences from the Buddhist perspective, we see that, in many ways, Marcie is indeed asking more of the universe—and of life—than it is able to give. As our earlier "Maimonidean" analysis would also affirm, Marcie simply expects life to conform to her needs and desires. She tells her therapist that "People just get on my nerves. Every little thing they do really annoys me. Like, if somebody gives me a dirty look, or acts like they're better than I am, it just drives me around the bend. I mean, nobody has a right to do that!"

Well, *who says* nobody has a right to give other people a "dirty look", or to act superior toward others? Cognitive therapists and Stoics alike would remind Marcie that the world is full of such insensitive types, and that we had better figure out how to live with that reality! So would the sages of Buddhism. As the 7th century Buddhist monk, Shantideva, puts it:

> ". . . even if one sees a friend or an enemy behaving badly, one can reflect that there are specific conditioning factors that determine this, and thereby remain happy . . . If it is their very nature to cause others distress, my anger towards those fools is as inappropriate as it would be towards fire for its nature to burn." (Perfection of Forbearance, in *The Bodhicaryavatara*, 33,39).

In this same work—which is actually a manual for the aspiring *bodhisattva*—Shantideva discusses how important it is to guard our "awareness" or "alertness" (*samprajanya*). He compares the undisciplined, unguarded mind to a "rutting elephant" on the rampage! Then Shantideva says,

> ". . . but if the roaming elephant, the mind, is tethered on every side by the cord of mindfulness, every danger subsides, [and] complete prosperity ensues." (The Guarding of Awareness, *The Bodhicaryavatara*, 2-3)

Our unfortunate friend, Marcie, seems to have allowed her mind to become untethered in just this way. It's not hard to understand why she tells her therapist, "I feel like I'm walking through life in a daze. Or maybe, a haze. It's like, I bounce from one feeling to another, like I'm a ping-pong ball." And Marcie is far from alone in feeling this way.

Marcie has also become excessively focused on *herself*, and her own needs and desires. In Buddhism, this is considered a profound error. Aside from the Buddhist belief that the independent "self" is an illusion—the concept of *anatman*—there is a practical issue involved. As Shantideva puts it,

> "All those who suffer in the world do so because of their desire for their own happiness. All those [who are] happy in the world are so because of their desire for the happiness of others." (from *The Bodhicaryavatara*, 8.129).

The Tibetan Buddhist monk, Chagdud Tulku, makes a similar point, in a manner that seems to fit Marcie very well:

". . . we need to begin by reducing our self-focus and self-important thoughts. To do so, we remind ourselves that we aren't the only ones who want to be happy—everyone does . . . Everyone has problems, many far worse than our own. As we contemplate this, our view expands to encompass the suffering of others. As our compassion deepens, our relentless self-focusing is reduced; we become more intent on helping others and better able to do so." (p. 16).

We can also analyze Marcie's predicament using the Buddhist concept of the "Eight Worldly Concerns." As B. Alan Wallace tells us, these involve *gain and loss; pleasure and pain; praise and blame;* and *fame and disgrace.* Wallace notes that "These are the concerns that pervade most people's daily lives . . . because they are mistaken for effective means to attain happiness and to avoid suffering." (p. 2). That is, many of us spend our time and energy seeking material gain; short-term pleasure; the praise of others; and the acknowledgement and publicity that comes with fame or notoriety. (If you want an example, think about the participants in those "reality TV" shows that dominate television and popular entertainment these days). Marcie, for example, hankers after luxury items, even though they provide only a "quick high" followed by a crash. She gets some transient pleasure—or at least, relief from her emotional pain—by abusing alcohol and marijuana, only to have the hollowness of her life hit home shortly after her drug-induced high. Furthermore, Marcie disturbs herself by fixating on what others say and do (". . . every little thing they do really annoys me . . ."), and on whether or not people praise or blame her (". . . like, if somebody gives me a dirty look, or acts like they're better than I am, it just drives me around the bend!"). Finally, Marcie's posting of provocative videos on Youtube is an example of the fruitless fixation on fame so common in today's pop culture. All that said, Wallace makes an important point about the "worldly concerns," noting that they are not "inherently bad":

> "It is not bad to buy a car, enjoy a fine meal, to be praised for one's work, or be respected by others. Rather, the reason for pointing them out is to reveal their essentially *transient nature and their impotence as means to lasting happiness.*" (*Tibetan Buddhism*, p. 3, italics added).

In this regard, Buddhism has important things to say about Marcie's avoiding the issues of "old age or dying." Shantideva, for example, taught that the *fear of death* colors and distorts our view of life, and leads us to all sorts of defensive but ultimately futile maneuvers—like drinking and drugging. As Prof. Jay Garfield notes, for Shantideva, the fear of death is what generates and animates "confusion, attachment, and aversion." These irrational mental states lead, in turn, to non-virtuous and self-defeating behaviors. Most of us are rarely aware of our fear of death, and many of us may actively deny or repress it. When we first become aware of how fleeting our existence is, this can be very distressing. But Buddhism tells us that the awareness of death opens an avenue of escape from the unenlightened life. By choosing to *cultivate virtue*, we can overcome our fear of death. As the Tibetan monk, Gen Rinpoche (Geshe Ngawang Dhargyey,1921-95) expresses it,

> "By maintaining awareness of death while alive, your life will spontaneously incline towards virtue and Dharma practice. Death will not come as a surprise and will bring neither fear nor regret." (http://dbc. dharmakara.net/GNDBiography.html).

In short, awareness of death is a doorway to the *cultivation of virtue*—which is the substance of Shantideva's "manual" for the aspiring Bodhisatva. We will explore this in detail in Chapter 5, on "Ethical Obligations and the Flourishing Life."

The Stoic Perspective

The essence of Stoic philosophy is well expressed by Marcus Aurelius: "Things do not touch the soul, for they are external and remain immovable; but our perturbations come only from the opinion which is within [us] . . ." And, as we have seen, this is mirrored in much of Buddhist philosophy—for example, "All that we are arises with our thoughts . . ." as written in the Dhammapada. So, what would the Stoics say of Marcie's sad situation?

They would undoubtedly join with both the Talmudic scholars and Buddhist sages in concluding that Marcie's "understanding" is severely hampered by a number of irrational beliefs. Let's consider Marcie's "Go along to get along" attitude, which sometimes leads her to behave (as she puts it) like "a door mat." Here we confront what at first glance seems to be a paradox within Stoic philosophy. On the one hand, the Stoics believe that it is our own *opinion* of events and people that lead us to feel angry or upset—*not* people or events themselves. This often leads Stoic philosophers to counsel patience and forbearance, in the face of provocative or obnoxious behavior. As Marcus Aurelius famously advises us,

> "Begin the morning by saying to yourself, I shall meet with the busybody, the ungrateful, arrogant, deceitful, envious, unsocial. All these things happen to them by reason of their ignorance of what is good

and evil . . . [but] I can neither be injured by any of
them . . . nor can I be angry with my kinsman, nor
hate him."

This is undoubtedly sage advice for Marcie, when she is
dealing with someone who is simply *annoying* her ("People just
get on my nerves . . . Like, if somebody gives me a dirty look or
acts like they're better than I am . . .").

On the other hand, the Stoics *do not* counsel cowardly
passivity, nor would they advise simply "turning the other cheek"
when faced with evil, injustice or outrageous behavior. In fact, the
Roman statesman and philosopher Seneca observed that, "Every
trouble that may come our way presses harder on the one who
has turned tail and is giving ground." (Letter XXVIII). Similarly,
philosopher William Irvine notes that the Stoics believed there are
times when responding to an insult is appropriate and necessary;
for example, if a student insults the teacher in front of the class,
the teacher must respond with appropriate action. Furthermore,
as Irvine notes, ". . . the Stoics also agree with modern social
reformers that we have a duty to fight against social injustice."
(p. 221). And so, it would be a serious mistake to call the Stoics
"fatalists", who think we must simply accept whatever befalls us.
At the same time, Irvine adds this important caveat:

> "The Stoics [believed] that *if we fail to transform
> ourselves*, then no matter how much we transform
> the society in which we live, we are unlikely to have
> a good life." (p.221, italics added).

And so, while the Stoics would admonish Marcie to stop
behaving like a "door mat"—reminding us of Hillel's question,
"If I am not for myself, who will be for me?"—they would also
see many other ways in which Marcie needs to "transform" herself

and her attitudes. Indeed, the Stoics would probably argue that before Marcie can genuinely act more assertively**, she must first *modify the way she reasons* about herself and others.

Marcie believes—or at least, she tries to convince herself—that she can find happiness through the acquisition of material things, such as "luxury items." The Stoics took a dim view of this notion—whereas, in our modern, Western culture, the idea remains alive and well (think about Madonna's popular song, "Material Girl"). Most Stoic philosophers believed that we ought to acquire just enough wealth and material possessions to live in modest and decent comfort—but not more than that. They also understood that a constant yearning or craving for material goods was bound to leave us disappointed in the long run. Epictetus asked, "What is it then that makes a man free and independent? For neither riches, nor consulship, nor the command of provinces . . . can make him so. Something else must be found." (Discourses, LXXXV). And what is this something else? Epictetus answers, "*The knowledge of living.*" And what kind of knowledge do we need? Seneca tells us,

> "It is in no man's power to have whatever he wants; but he has it in his power not to wish for what he hasn't got; and cheerfully make the most of the things that do come his way." (Letter CXXIII).

Perhaps the most troubling element in Marcie's emotional life is her stark dependency on others. Of course, we all depend on others to some degree—for example, we depend on doctors for our health care, or the police, for our protection. But Marcie "puts up" with Bob's sarcasm and lack of affection because she sees him as a "security blanket." Furthermore, Marcie sees her happiness in terms of how others behave toward her. Again, this is true of all of us, to some degree—nobody appreciates an insult or a smack in the face!—but Marcie allows herself to be driven "around the bend" by such trivial events as somebody's giving her "a dirty look." From the Stoic perspective, it's no wonder Marcie feels like "a leaf being blown around in the wind." She *allows* herself to be blown around, *because she does not anchor herself to a set of rational values and beliefs.* As Epictetus observes, "Because of our neglect to study the proper valuation of the phenomena of existence, we always exaggerate, and represent things to ourselves greater than the reality." For example, Marcie exaggerates the power others have to drive her "around the bend." In reality, as William Irvine puts it,

> "Others may have it in their power to affect how
> and even whether you live, but they do not . . . have
> it in their power to ruin your life. Only you can ruin
> it, by failing to live in accordance with the correct
> values." (Irvine, op cit, p. 221).

Similarly, Epictetus taught, "If you wish for good, receive it from yourself." He taught that "we should be prepared to be sufficient unto ourselves, and to bear our own company." (*Discourses*, LXXVIII). Yet, like Marcie, many unhappy people desperately seek happiness through the attention or affection of others. This doesn't mean that the Stoics were a bunch of anti-social misfits or hermits. They recognized that friendship and good company were wonderful enhancements to "the good life." But to regard the company or affection of others as *essential to our happiness* is to hand our lives over to forces beyond our control. This, the Stoics firmly renounced.

At the same time that Marcie seeks happiness and security through others, she is—somewhat paradoxically—almost entirely focused on *herself.* She is preoccupied with her needs, her feelings, and her sadly shrunken world. Now, while the

Stoics valued self-reliance and independence, they also believed in something beyond our own mundane selves. They called this "something" by various names—sometimes "Logos", sometimes "God", sometimes "Nature." For the Stoics, we achieve the "good life" not by obsessing over our own needs, but by *attuning ourselves to Nature*, and accepting life on its own terms. (Here we see immediate affinities with the Buddhist ideal of avoiding *tanha*—that is, not asking more of the world than it can possibly deliver). The Stoics believed, in effect, that by following Nature, we were following God—a concept we find many centuries later in the views of the philosopher, Baruch Spinoza. Furthermore, the Stoics saw Nature as essentially the *principle of reason*. Thus, Marcus Aurelius tells us that, ". . . the same act is according to Nature and according to Reason."

And how are we to follow Nature, according to the Stoics? Philosopher Keith Seddon sums it up this way:

> "First, we must pay attention to our own actions so
> that we respond appropriately; and second, we must
> pay attention to the world in which our actions take
> effect . . ." (p. 22, Epictetus' *Handbook*).

This is close in spirit to the Buddhist idea of "mindfulness" or being "awake". It also has affinities with the mystical side of Judaism, called *Hasidism*, which emphasizes that communion with God may be achieved even in mundane acts, such as eating, walking, or doing business (Joseph Dan, *The Teachings of Hasidism*).

Another aspect of "following Nature" for the Stoics involved accepting what life brings us, in all its pleasures and pains. In fact, Epictetus thought of life as a kind of "festival", arranged for our benefit by God! As Seddon puts it, this festival is ". . . something that we can live through joyously, able to put up with any hardships that befall us because we have our eye on the larger spectacle that is taking place." (Seddon, p. 24).

Again, we need to be careful here: the Stoics are not saying that we ought to "put up" with evil or injustice without lifting a finger! On the contrary, we should exert our best efforts to make life better for ourselves and others. But once we have done so, we may need to accept that the world is, well—still very much the world, with all its injustices and imperfections. For example, the philosopher Chrysippus taught that disease is an inevitable consequence of the universe ". . . having the particular constitution that it happens to have." (Seddon, p. 107). We can continue to think up ways of making things better, of course—for example, by doing our best to diagnose and cure disease. But we are under no obligation to make ourselves miserable when we fail in this endeavor, or to imagine that it is in our power to cure every disease!

Synthesis and Commentary

Marcie's story brings to mind Wordsworth's famous sonnet, which begins,

> *The world is too much with us; late and soon,*
> *Getting and spending, we lay waste our powers;*
> *Little we see in Nature that is ours . . ."*

Notice that for Wordsworth, as for the sages within our three traditions, it is *we*—not others—who "lay waste our powers." Like Marcie, we rely too much on "the world" and its material preoccupations. Wordsworth also picks up the theme—more prominent in Buddhism and Stoicism than in Judaism—of our alienation from "Nature."

All three of our spiritual traditions would view Marcie's predicament as stemming from both cognitive errors and from a failure to "keep faith" with certain foundational values. Thus, Marcie mistakenly believes she can "get through" life by escaping from her problems, rather than by forthrightly dealing with them. She believes that by accumulating "stuff", she will somehow find happiness, and that her emotional well-being is really in the hands of others. Marcie has also "broken faith" on the three levels described by Rabbi Yosef Tropper; that is, in her *relationship with herself; her relationship with others; and her relationship with God or Nature.* We see this in her lack of self-care and refusal to be an advocate for her own interests; her dependent and "clinging" relationships with others; and in her alienation from any principle that transcends her own sphere of self-involvement.

This doesn't mean we should "blame" or condemn Marcie—much less look down on her. In her struggle to find "the good life", Marcie is, so to speak, *all of us.* In Sanskrit, we find the term, *shubharthi*, meaning 'seeker of well being.' Marcie is surely that—as are we all. And, as a psychiatrist, I can point to many factors in Marcie's early childhood experience that help explain her difficulties in making her way through life. For example, Marcie described her home life as follows:

> *"We all sort of competed for mom and dad's attention, like little sparrows. You had to get mom or dad to notice you, and kind of be on your side, or you'd get out-maneuvered by big sister or big brother. And, there was never really enough to go around in our house—not enough food, not enough love. If you got on mom or dad's bad side, you'd get smacked down pretty quick—not physically, but with a dirty look, or a snide remark."*

Any child growing up in this kind of "survival of the fittest" environment—in which you survive by currying favor and avoiding punishment—is bound to have difficulties as an adult. Marcie's clinging and dependent relationships with the men in her life are almost certainly related to the insecurity and lack of nurturance she felt as a child—starved not only for food, but also for love.

At the same time, the sages of our three traditions would not let Marcie off the hook. They would acknowledge that she started out with a "bad hand" in life, but would gently suggest that she needs to play her cards far more wisely. So, too, with the cognitive-behavioral therapists, who argue that we are all capable of overcoming the baneful effects of a deprived or unloving childhood. As Drs. Albert Ellis and Robert Harper put it in their classic, *A Guide to Rational Living,*

> "No matter what a person's past history may be, or how his parents, teachers, and other early associates may have helped him to become emotionally disturbed, he only remains disturbed because he still believes some of the unrealistic and illogical thoughts which he originally imbibed. To become undisturbed, therefore, it is only necessary that he see what his present irrational self-indoctrinations are, and that he energetically and consistently work at de-indoctrinating . . . himself . . ." (pp. 50-51).

What is required, then, is *mental discipline*, or what the Buddhists would call, "right thinking." The great medieval sage, Maimonides, put it this way:

> "The more one is disciplined, the less one is affected by both extremes, good and bad; so that when one is favored by great fortune in this world, one does not get [overly] excited . . . And when great misfortune and tribulations [come], one is neither startled

nor terrified, but tolerates them well." (from *The Preservation of Youth*).

We alluded earlier to Shantideva's image of the "elephants of the mind", whose rampages causes us so much distress. An even more vivid image was provided by the Buddha himself, who likened unwholesome thinking to wearing a dead snake around your neck! (*The Heart of the Buddha's Teaching*, p. 62). (This image is particularly interesting, given that the founder of the Red Cross, Clara Barton, referred to her bouts of severe depression as those, "thin black snakes.")

In the next chapter, we'll examine in detail how our "dead snakes" can cause us a great deal of suffering, and how we can begin to free ourselves from these serpents of our own minds.

**This differs somewhat from Maimonides' view that by first changing our *behavior*, we can actually modify our beliefs and feelings. This "behavioral" view is actually more consonant with modern cognitive-behavioral theories than some of the Stoics' views.

Chapter 3

THINKING AND SUFFERING

Judaism

"Who fills his mind with Torah clears it of fear and folly."

—Rabbi Chanina Sgan HaKohanim

"Rather than falling into despair over his shortcomings, [one] must seek out positive elements in the totality of his being and judge himself favorably on that basis."

—Nahman of Bratslav, *Liqqutei Moharan* 282

"Of all the tyrants in the world, our own attitudes are the fiercest warlords."

—Rabbi Dr. Joseph Gelberman

Buddhism

"The moment you know how your suffering came to be, you are already on the path of release from it."

—The Buddha, *Samyutta Nikaya*

"Hell is the reflection of mind's delusion, of angry thoughts and intentions and the harmful words and actions they produce."

—Chagdud Tulku

"It's our failure to understand the essential nature of an emotion as it arises that gets us into trouble. Once we do, the emotion tends to dissolve."

—Chagdud Tulku

Stoicism

"It is not he who gives abuse . . . who offends us; but the view that we take of these things as insulting or hurtful . . . Try therefore, in the first place, not to be bewildered by appearances.

—Epictetus (Discourses)

"When . . . you see someone pale with worry . . . this man is disordered in his desires and aversions."

—Epictetus (Discourses)

". . . it is in the soul's power to preserve its own quiet and calm, and not to judge pain to be an evil; for every judgment, impulse, desire or aversion is within . . ."

—Marcus Aurelius (Meditations, VIII, 28)

Vignette: Forrest's Failings

Forrest, a 35-year-old married father of two, was the picture of success. Handsome, brilliant, and a "rising star" in the realm of corporate finance, Forrest seemed to have the world on a string. His wife, Katya, was a beautiful and successful ballet teacher, and the two of them were justly proud of their very bright, 6-year-old son and 3-year-old daughter. But for all this worldly success, Forrest was a seething cauldron of resentment and self-deprecation.

He entered psychotherapy complaining that "The story of my life is the title of that old Rolling Stones song, 'I Can't Get No Satisfaction.'" Forrest described himself as "a self-confessed control freak" who found it hard to tolerate any "slip ups" on the part of his subordinates and colleagues. Although he was considered a "genius" at his corporate headquarters, Forrest was also known for his hot temper and sharp words, when he felt others were not "performing up to snuff." He also reacted with intense anger when criticized by his more senior colleagues, sometimes "getting right up in their face," insulting them, and nearly coming to blows.

In his psychotherapy, Forrest revealed that, "I'm hard on others, I'll admit—but I'm even harder on myself." Indeed, Forrest considered himself "kind of a jerk" who had made good despite his own shortcomings. "People see this big, hot-shot, success story when they look at me. But I think I should have achieved a hell of a lot more, at my age. I don't consider myself a success, even though I've made a lot of money and have a nice house and a beautiful wife. I had always seen myself as someone who would own his own company, maybe create some new start-ups that would really shake things up in the finance world—you know, maybe wind up like Warren Buffett or Bill Gates. I figured by now, we'd have a house in the Hamptons, maybe another on the Cape. Instead, I feel like I'm kind of a flop. I'm running on a treadmill, performing for people I can't stand, and who are constantly trying to undermine me. I can't even tell you how much these clowns at work piss me off!" He added that he spent much of the time feeling anxious and "wired", often worrying about failing in his work, or being criticized by his superiors.

Forrest's sessions were filled with vitriolic rants about particular colleagues or subordinates, whom he named without hesitation. Despite his seeming contempt for others, Forrest described himself as "cut off" and "lonely", even around his wife and children. He noted, "I don't really have any close friends. I love Katya and the kids, but I just don't seem to connect with them. I don't think they "get" me. Katya can't understand why I want to grab the gold ring. She thinks I've done fine and should be happy with what we have. Of course, she's one of these "artsy" types, you know. She'd probably be happy living in Greenwich Village and teaching ballet in some crummy studio for a hundred bucks a week. Me, I want to *be* somebody." Forrest admitted to feeling "under-appreciated" by his wife, and added, "Sometimes I think she loves the kids more than she loves me. Then again, who could blame her?" Forrest acknowledged that he and Katya ". . . hardly ever do much in bed anymore," and that "I think she mostly just puts up with me."

Forrest was the youngest of three children. He described his parents as "pretty remote" and "always expecting perfection from us kids." He characterized his father as "a failed writer" who took out his frustrations on his wife and children. Forrest described his mother as "kind of a people-pleaser, always trying to keep my dad happy by doing what he told her to do. I used to be my mother's "support group" and she sort of relied on me for a shoulder to cry on. I guess I was her favorite, since she would take me into her confidence more than she would my brother and sister. At times, I felt more like the parent than the kid, with my mom. I mean, she was pretty needy." At the same time, he related that his mother was "always telling me I could do better" and "hardly ever gave me credit, even when I got top grades in school." Forrest described making strenuous efforts to please his father while in elementary school, but becoming "hostile" and "very competitive with dad" in his teen years.

Forrest, from the Jewish perspective

As reflected in our opening epigram from Nahman of Bratslav (one should ". . . seek out positive elements in the totality of his being and judge himself favorably on that basis"), Judaism emphasizes the importance of *self-esteem* and self-respect. At the same time, *respect for others* is a foundational value in Judaism, as expressed in the Talmudic teaching, "Whoever shames another in public is like one who sheds blood." (Bava Metzia 58b). Forrest, alas, has serious problems in both spheres: self-respect *and* respect for others. The two are clearly linked: a person who considers himself "a jerk" is not likely to treat others with kindness and respect—a concept known as *k'vod habryot* (respect for human dignity). (*K'vod habryot* is an outgrowth of another foundational belief in Judaism; namely, that all human beings—Jews and non-Jews alike—are created in the Divine image).

The neo-Orthodox rabbi, Sampson Raphael Hirsch (1808-88) points to the link between self-esteem and respect for others: "First, become a blessing to yourself, so that you may be a blessing to others." As psychologists have long known, self-esteem must lay the foundation for the esteem of others; otherwise, one's self-hatred seeps into and infects one's relationships with nearly everyone else. Forrest's self-deprecating comments remind us of Groucho Marx's quip, "I refuse to join any club that would have me as a member!" (Ironically, Groucho seems to have imbibed not only the Judaic, but also the Stoic tradition, as this quote attributed to him clearly suggests: "Each morning when I open my eyes I say to myself: I, not events, have the power to make me happy or unhappy today. I can choose which it shall be. Yesterday is dead, tomorrow hasn't arrived yet. I have just one day, today, and I'm going to be happy in it."—from *The Essential Groucho: Writings For By And About Groucho Marx*).

Also evident in Forrest's world-view is the sense that he has never lived up to his own (rather grandiose) expectations; that he has never acquired enough power or wealth ("like Warren Buffett"); and that he must always be "in control." Forrest also seems to think that he has the right to react with anger when others either under-perform, or dare to criticize him. Finally, he has no hesitation in speaking ill of those he looks down upon as "clowns", even using their names in his therapy sessions. Taken as a whole, Forrest's outlook flies in the face of Judaic philosophy and ethics—and is almost guaranteed to leave him feeling lonely and unloved, even in his own home. And, as we'll see, there are cognitive distortions associated with many of these ethical lapses.

Let's start with the acquisition of power, wealth and influence that Forrest seems to crave. The Judaic view is that real "power" consists in our ability to master our own emotions and impulses. "Who is mighty?" the Talmud asks, and answers, "He who subdues his passions." (Pirke Avot 4:1). And in what does *wealth* consist? In the Judaic tradition, wealth does not mean becoming as rich as Croesus (or Bill Gates), or having a mansion in the Hamptons. The Talmud asks, "Who is rich?" and answers, "He who rejoices in his portion." (Pirke Avot 4:1). Thus, as Rabbi Dan Roth observes, the Talmud teaches us that "wealth" is really a *state of mind*, and ". . . an internal quality emanating from the core of [one's] being." [p. 82, *Relevance: Pirke Avos for the Twenty-First century*]. Rabbi Roth continues to explore this theme, and in doing so, brilliantly analyzes Forrest's entire predicament:

> ". . . increasing one's possessions will never bring happiness because happiness depends on having one's emotional needs fulfilled, and material objects cannot satisfy emotional needs. Happiness depends on feeling connected to other people and enjoying close relationships with them, feeling a strong sense

of self-worth, and deriving meaning and lasting enjoyment from life. None of these emotional needs can be fully satisfied by pursuing wealth or purchasing objects." (Roth, p. 86, *Relevance: Pirke Avos for the Twenty-First century*).

Indeed, the Jewish tradition is somewhat suspicious of great wealth, fearing that it often brings more sorrow than pleasure. As the 11th century philosopher, Joseph ibn Pakuda put it, "Wealth is affliction disguised as a good."

There is another sense in which wealth is a "state of mind" in the Judaic tradition, and this relates to the rabbinical view of *knowledge*. The Talmud teaches us that, "If you have knowledge you have everything." (Nedarim 40b). This passage goes on to say,

> ". . . if you don't have knowledge, what have you got? If you acquired knowledge, what else do you need? If you have not acquired knowledge, what good are all your possessions?" (from *Ein Yaakov*, translated by AY Finkel).

> Another Talmudic passage links *wisdom and wealth*, since ". . . when you acquire wisdom you will also acquire wealth, [because when you are wise, you are happy with your lot, and you feel rich . . ."] (Bava Batra 25b)

Forrest sees himself as a "flop", apparently because he hasn't achieved his professional and financial goals (though his low self-esteem almost certainly has unconscious roots in his early family life—more on this anon). In contrast, the Judaic tradition looks at apparent failure as a kind of *opportunity*, not as an occasion to hit oneself over the head. Thus, Rabbi Raymond Beyda observes that

> "Even failing can be positive. In order to grow and reach new heights *Hashem* [God] confronts the human being with obstacles and tests . . . The test is an opportunity to grow from the situation—and even failure presents a positive side. If you analyze your defeat you can usually discover a positive learning experience . . . Today when you get hit with something that you see as failure—stop. Say to yourself, "I am certainly disappointed that I did not succeed, but the wisdom I have gained from past experiences . . . makes me feel that perhaps even now I am misinterpreting these events. In the end it will all work out and I will be a better performer going forward." (Reflections, 2010, by <u>Rabbi Raymond Beyda</u>, **<u>Torah.org</u>**.)

This view is also quite compatible with both Stoicism and the philosophy of cognitive-behavioral therapy, and Albert Ellis's REBT.

Forrest's habit of reacting angrily to others—often with "sharp words" or "getting right up in their face"—is in stark contrast to the Judaic view of accepting criticism, and of controlling one's anger. In Pirke Avot (6:6), we find a listing of 48 traits required for the acquisition of Torah, among which is "loving reproof." Of course, very few of us rise to that lofty standard, and most of us really don't enjoy being criticized! Nevertheless, as Rabbi Reuven P. Bulka has observed, "Reproof can raise the individual out of stagnation towards greater heights of achievement." (Bulka, *Chapters of the Sages*, 1993, p. 257).

We will deal with the problem of anger in detail, in chapter 9. For now, suffice it to say that Forrest would do well to heed the words of Ben Zoma, in Pirke Avot (4:1): "One who is slow to anger is better than the mighty, and one who rules over one's spirit is better than one who conquers a city."

There is another Talmudic maxim that has relevance to Forrest's predicament. In Pirke Avot (2:16), we read, *"Rabbi Yehoshua said: An evil eye, the evil inclination, and hatred of others (lit., of the creations) remove a person from the world."* In Forrest's seething resentment, envy, and contempt, we find an "eye" that sees mainly evil in the world. It is this *attitude*—not the success or wealth of others—that "removes" Forrest from the pleasures and blessings of this world. As Rabbi Dovid Rosenfeld eloquently puts it:

> "Rather than being happy with others' good fortune and accomplishments, [the jealous person] begrudges them what is theirs. And such a jealous person does not have a life—not his own one at least. He pines away wishing he were someone else—that he had his fellow's talents, success, popularity, or prestige. And one who wishes he were someone else will fail to live up to his own talents—or even recognize what they are. He will "remove" himself from the world, not living and enjoying the life G-d has granted him, but rather wasting away in his greed and self-pity." (*Pirkei Avos*, Torah.org)

Since the relationship between man and wife is central to the Judaic idea of "the good life," we should say a bit about Forrest's relationship with Katya. Forrest admits feeling "under-appreciated" by his wife, and tells the therapist, "Sometimes I think she loves the kids more than she loves me. Then again, who could blame her?" He acknowledges that there is little sexual intimacy between them, and we sense a wide, emotional rift between Forrest and Katya—probably fueled by Forrest's insecurity and poor self-concept. All of this reflects the absence of what Judaism calls, *shalom bayit*—roughly translated, "peaceful marriage" or "domestic peace." Talmudic and rabbinical sources place a good deal of responsibility on the husband, when it comes to maintaining *shalom bayit*. In a work called, *Iggeret ha-Kodesh*—a thirteenth-century Hebrew text traditionally attributed to the philosopher, Nahmanides (1194-1270 CE)—we find a moving description of the husband's responsibility in the marriage:

> "Great is the husband's obligation to nurture the relationship of love and of closeness between a husband and his wife, every day, every year, in every circumstance, in every attitudinal environment, until the end of his life." (From Forsyth, http://www.shemayisrael.com/rabbiforsythe/shalombayis/kavod.htm#6)

It seems clear that Forrest has not been able to fulfill this role, and that his alienation from Katya is yet another reason why his life remains so empty. Of course, both man and wife share responsibility for making the marriage "work."

Finally, the Judaic tradition would take a very dim view of Forrest's willingness to "badmouth" others, and to dismiss them as "clowns." This falls under the rubric of *lashon hara* ("evil tongue") and *motzi shem ra* ("giving another a bad name"). The Rabbis of the Talmud emphasized that such derogatory speech is not merely "bad manners"—*it tears at the very fabric of society, and harms all that it touches.* As the Talmud puts it, "Why is the evil tongue called the thrice-slaying tongue? Because it slays the person saying it, the hearer, and the person spoken about."

(Arachin 15b). Indeed, the Rabbis considered it wrong even to *listen* to derogatory speech, much less to spread it. One of the very few exceptions is when a loved one is in need of emotional support and decides to "ventilate" about someone who has upset him or her. We may then listen to *lashon hara*, in order to allow the distressed person a bit of catharsis—but even then, we should do our best to guide our loved one back to a more temperate state of mind.

The Buddhist Perspective

As we've seen in our earlier discussions, the Buddhist world-view sees all of us as part of an interconnected and interdependent whole; and as part of a vast chain of causality stretching back through eternity. If this all sounds very nebulous and mystical, consider how incredibly *self-focused* Forrest has become. Every issue he brings up in therapy revolves around *his* needs, *his* goals, and *his* dissatisfactions. Of course, we are all concerned deeply with our own desires and frustrations, and therapy is a good place to "ventilate" about these issues. But from the Buddhist perspective, an overly-intense self-focus is a *cognitive error* that creates suffering within us. To counteract this, we must put our own desires, woes and "attachments" in a much broader context. As the scholar Robert Thurman puts it,

> "Think about . . . the thousands of ways in which we can be knocked down by illness, pain, injury, sorrow, death. Why do we take this step now? Because meditation on the prevalence of suffering helps us tolerate our pains by putting them into perspective." (Thurman, *Infinite Life*, p. 170).

From this universal point of view, is Forrest's sense of disgruntled entitlement really justified? Given all the genuine misfortune in the world—famine, disease, floods and hurricanes!—is lacking a house in the Hamptons really so terrible? Forrest describes himself as a "control freak" who finds it hard to tolerate any "slip-ups" on the part of his subordinates and colleagues—and, no doubt, Forrest is equally hard on himself. Like many of us, Forrest upsets himself with petty, material "attachments", and the need to control external events and individuals. From the Buddhist perspective, this is a profound error. As Chagdud Tulku puts it,

> "We often think the only way to create happiness is to . . . control the outer circumstances of our lives . . . or to get rid of everything that bothers us. But the real problem lies in our reaction to those circumstances. *What we have to change is the mi nd and the way it experiences reality.*" (Tulku, pp. 7-8, italics added).

Forrest's self-focus also narrows his field of spiritual vision. He is so preoccupied with every little thing that annoys him, or with his supposed failings, that he can't see the infinitely bigger picture of life and death. Again, Chagdud Tulku comments:

> "Not knowing when we'll die, we need to develop an appreciation for and acceptance of what we have, while we have it, rather than continuing to find fault with our experience and seeking, incessantly, to fulfill our desires." (Tulku, p. 10).

In Buddhism, we are taught to avoid the "ten unwholesome deeds", including physical, verbal and mental misdeeds. Before exploring this issue in Forrest's case, let's recall that Buddhism—like

Judaism and Stoicism—emphasizes *ethical action* as the very essence of the good or "flourishing" life. Kindness and altruistic acts are particularly valued in the Mahayana tradition. Recall, for example, the comment of the Dalai Lama, on summarizing the essence of Shantideva's teachings, and indeed all of Mahayana Buddhism: "The only purpose of my existence is to be used by others and to serve others." One way in which we fulfill this purpose is through what Santideva calls, "forbearance." Essentially, this means *bearing with others' failings, and restraining our anger and animosity.* Shantideva writes,

> "One's mind finds no peace, neither enjoys pleasure or delight, nor goes to sleep . . . while the dart of hatred is stuck in the heart . . . even friends shrink from him . . . there is no sense in which someone prone to anger is well off." (*Bodhicaryavatara*, Perfection of Forbearance 3-5)

The application of this point to Forrest's life—he, of the sharp words and fiery temper!—hardly needs elaboration.

The dark, mirror-image of the ethically-fulfilled life is represented in the "Ten Unwholesome Deeds" described by B. Alan Wallace. The first three unwholesome deeds are *physical actions*, such as stealing or taking another's life; the next four are *verbal*, such as lying or engaging in abusive speech; and the final three are *mental* acts, such as a maintaining a mind-set of avarice or malice. It is apparent that Forrest has allowed himself to indulge in several of these unwholesome deeds, such as insulting his colleagues when criticized, or engaging in "vitriolic rants" about the "clowns" he sees as undermining him. The Buddhist concept of verbal abuse has obvious affinities with the rabbinical term, *lashon hara* ("evil tongue"), and is described by Wallace as follows: "If one speaks with the intention to inflict harm, this is abuse; and as we know, this may bring greater suffering to another person than physical injury." (Wallace, p. 97). (Here we are reminded of the Talmudic teaching that shaming another person in public is akin to "spilling blood").

Finally, there is the issue of Forrest's poor self-concept and low self-esteem. Here, too, Shantideva's observation is relevant. He speaks of those ". . . who injure even their own dear selves . . ." and asks, ". . . how could they have a care for the [personhood] of other people?" We may understand "self-injury" not merely in the physical sense (which we saw in Marcie's history in chapter 2), but also in the psychological and spiritual sense; for example, when Forrest describes himself as "kind of a jerk." Here, too, we are reminded of the Judaic view that links self-esteem with the ability to esteem others. Thus, in *Pirke Avot*, we are told, "Let your friend's honor be as dear to you as your own." (2:15). It is almost axiomatic that if you have no self-respect—if you do not honor yourself—you will not be able to honor others. To this, Shantideva would have assented readily.

The Stoic Perspective

If ever a person were "bewildered by appearances" and "disordered in his desires and aversions"—to recall the words of Epictetus—it is surely our friend, Forrest. In what sense does Forrest reflect these problems? Let's look at the context of Epictetus' first comment. He writes,

> "Remember that it is not he who gives abuse or blows who affronts; but the view we take of these things as insulting. When, therefore, any one provokes you, be assured that it is your own opinion which provokes you. Try, therefore, in the

first place, *not to be bewildered by appearances.* For
if you once gain time and respite, you will more
easily command yourself." (italics added, from the
Discourses, LXXX)

Forrest, let's recall, believes that those around him are causing
him tremendous distress and anger ("I can't even tell you how
much these clowns piss me off!"). Yet from the Stoic perspective,
this view reflects a misinterpretation of reality—that is, being
"bewildered by appearances." Like the cognitively-oriented
therapists—especially, Dr. Albert Ellis—the Stoics would point
out that it is Forrest's own *distorted and irrational cognitions* that
are causing him to become "pissed off." For example, Forrest may
believe, "Nobody has the right to criticize me!" or "Everybody
ought to approve of everything I do, or else they are ignorant
clowns!" But where is it written that we ought to be immune
from criticism, or that we must be rewarded with everybody's
praise? Furthermore, because Forrest allows himself to become
upset in the face of criticism, he loses "command" of himself, and
becomes insulting and verbally abusive. This, of course, does not
win him many friends, or allow him to "flourish" in his life.

Epictetus also observes that, "When . . . you see someone
pale with worry . . . this man is disordered in his desires and
aversions." What does Epictetus mean by this, and how does it
apply to Forrest? Epictetus makes his observation in the context
of discussing *anxiety*, and what causes it. He writes,

"When I see any one anxious, I say, what does this
man mean? Unless he *wanted something or other not
in his own power*, how could he still be anxious? A
musician, for instance, feels no anxiety while he is
singing by himself; but when he appears upon the
stage he does, even if his voice be ever so good . . .

> For what he wishes is not only to sing well, but
> likewise to gain applause. But this is not in his own
> power." (*Discourses*, Book II).

Forrest tells his therapist that he spends much of the time feeling anxious and "wired", often worrying about failing in his work, or being criticized by his superiors. Like many of us, Forrest is anxious because he wants "more than the universe can deliver", to hark back to the Buddhist concept of *tanha*. He wants to control what nobody can control: the opinions and behaviors of others. Forrest describes himself as a "control freak" who finds it hard to tolerate any "slip-ups" on the part of his subordinates and colleagues. But he is no more in control of these "slip-ups" than he is of his boss's approval.

Yes, the Stoics would admit: Forrest is, to some degree, capable of controlling his *own* slip ups—but even here, he reasons irrationally. He is "disordered" in his aversion to his own perceived failings. This is probably owing to Forrest's irrational perfectionism—something psychoanalysts would term a "punitive superego." The Stoics—while encouraging self-discipline—were well aware that no one always achieves perfection in virtue or behavior. And when we fall short, as we must, Marcus Aurelius wisely advised,

> "Be not disgusted, nor discouraged, nor dissatisfied,
> if you do not succeed in doing everything according
> to right principles; but when you have failed, return
> back again [to those principles] . . ." (*Meditations*)

Epictetus went even further in counseling against the habit of "blaming":

> "It is the action of an uninstructed person to reproach
> others for his own misfortune; of one entering upon

instruction to reproach himself; and one perfectly instructed to reproach neither others nor himself."

Perhaps the Stoic concept of "controlling what we can control" is best summed up in a metaphor from Cicero (106 BCE-43 BCE), the Roman statesman and philosopher. In his work, *De Finibus*, Cicero uses the analogy of an archer shooting an arrow at a target. As psychotherapist Donald Robertson observes,

> "[The archer's] ultimate wish is to hit the target, but he can only do everything within his power to shoot his arrow straight; and so, shooting straight, as opposed to actually hitting the target, must be his primary concern . . . [A]nd so it is with life in general." (from *The Philosophy of Cognitive-Behavioural Therapy (CBT)*, 2010).

Finally, the Stoics saw man's task as one of living in harmony with Nature, or with "the way things are." In this regard, Marcus Aurelius taught that, "Nothing will happen to [us] which is not conformable to the nature of the universe." In contrast, Forrest seems to rail against the world and its perceived injustices—for example, against the "clowns" who are constantly trying to "undermine" his efforts. In discussing the Stoic philosopher, Seneca, Alain de Botton notes that, insofar as we can ever attain wisdom, it is by,

> ". . . learning not to aggravate the world's obstinacy through our own responses, through spasms of rage, self-pity, anxiety, bitterness, self-righteousness and paranoia . . . Philosophy must reconcile us to the true dimensions of reality, and so spare us, if not frustration itself, then at least its panoply of

pernicious accompanying emotions." (from *The Consolations of Philosophy*, p. 81).

Synthesis and Commentary

In a recent New York Times article (4/10/12), Frank Bruni described the life of the legendary chef, Craig Claiborne, in these terms:

> "He had fans, friends, and fabulous kitchens . . . but . . . he frequently comes across as fearful, irritable, lonely and depressed . . . His tale is a sad reminder: happiness has less to do with achievement than with perspective. And sometimes, the person inside a life, storied or otherwise, is least able to savor it."

This description also fits Forrest very well—a man who, despite his evident talents, admits he "can't get no satisfaction" in life. It's no wonder: his fundamental lack of self-esteem and self-respect have effectively "kneecapped" his ability to relate to others and to find pleasure in his own substantial accomplishments. He holds others to nearly impossible standards of performance, and is even harder on himself. In this, Forrest is hardly alone. As the writer Thornton Wilder once commented,

> ". . . many an American is breaking his life on an excessive demand for the perfect, the absolute, and the boundless, in realms where it is accorded to few—in love and friendship, for example. The doctrines of moderation and the golden mean may have flourished in Rome and in China . . . but they do not flourish here . . ." (from a lecture given at Harvard).

Psychotherapists will readily see the roots of Forrest's problems in his early family environment. Assuming his account to be accurate, we learn that Forrest's parents were emotionally aloof and "always expecting perfection" from him and his siblings. Forrest was, in a sense, "parentified" by a mother who relied on him for emotional support, while rarely giving him any real nurturance or affirmation. Forrest seems to have internalized his parents' perfectionistic expectations, while failing to develop a firm sense of himself as a competent person, worthy of love and respect. Forrest's "hostile" and "competitive" relationship with his father seems to be recapitulated in the way he now relates to his supervisors at work.

But—important though these psychodynamic issues are to clinicians—they are actually peripheral to the "core" of the three spiritual traditions we are exploring. This is owing, in part, to the strong emphasis on *cognitive distortions* in Judaism, Buddhism, and Stoicism; and, in part, to their focus on *ethical behavior* as the only lasting foundation for "the good life." Indeed, it's fair to sum up the "JuBuSto" perspective on Forrest along these lines: *Whatever the baneful effects of his early childhood, Forrest's unhappiness is largely self-created. He is the unwitting victim of his own irrational perceptions and beliefs, and of his failure to find a sound ethical framework for his life and behavior.*

To be sure, the Judaic tradition acknowledges the prominent role of early family influences on the personality of the child. Thus, the Talmud wisely observes that, "What a child says on the street, the parents said at home." (Sukka, 56b). But the rabbinical tradition does not let us off the hook, even if we have been exposed to inappropriate or inadequate parenting. We are still responsible, as adults, for *thinking rationally.* (In this respect, there is a deep and fundamental connection between Judaism and cognitive-behavioral forms of therapy, particularly the approach of the late Dr. Albert Ellis, termed "REBT.")

From the Judaic perspective, we are not merely "victims" of our past—we are active shapers of our present and future. For example, *we have an affirmative obligation to find the good, as well as the evil, within ourselves.* Thus, the Talmud tells us, "Do not consider yourself wicked." (Pirke Avot 2:18). Indeed, as the Hasidic sage, Nahman of Breslov, counseled, "Rather than falling into despair over his shortcomings, [one] must seek out [the] positive elements in the totality of his being and judge himself favorably on that basis." (Lieber, 1995, p. 27)

Judaism does not countenance an unrealistically "rosy" self-concept, nor does it tolerate narcissistic grandiosity. Rather, it urges us to seek a *reasoned balance* in our self-assessment. Thus, Rabbi Simcha Bunam used to say, "Every person should have two pockets. In one, [there should be a note that says] . . . 'for my sake was the world created.' In the second, [there should be a note that says] . . . 'I am dust and ashes.'" When we are feeling really "down" on ourselves, we are admonished to pull out and read the first note. When we are feeling smug and self-satisfied, we should take out the note that says, 'I am dust and ashes.' (Telushkin, 2006, p. 239)

In contrast, Forrest seems to swing like a pendulum between a grandiose sense of entitlement and the belief that he is "a jerk." It's almost as if he repeatedly pulls out the "wrong note" at the wrong time, thus fueling either his narcissism or his self-contempt. (Psychiatrists, by the way, have long hypothesized that beneath the outward "golden armor" of the narcissist, there lies a soft, underbelly of insecurity and self-contempt).

At the same time, Forrest's obnoxious behavior is totally inconsistent with Talmudic injunctions against humiliating or insulting others. Rabbi Yitzchok Isaac Silver explains the incalculable damage we can do when we verbally abuse another person:

"People sometimes mistakenly think that words are of little substance and cannot cause real harm. However, the [Talmud] states that in several ways, hurting others with words is a more severe transgression than cheating them financially. Money taken fraudulently can be returned; hurt feelings cannot always be restored. Fraud affects only the person's belongings . . . [whereas] hurting with words . . . *affects the person himself.*" (from *The Code of Jewish Conduct*)

From the Buddhist and Stoic perspectives, Forrest's predicament is summed up in Chagdud Tulku's observation that

"We often think the only way to create happiness is to . . . control the outer circumstances of our lives . . . or to get rid of everything that bothers us. But the real problem lies in our reaction to those circumstances. *What we have to change is the mind and the way it experiences reality.*" (Tulku, pp. 7-8, italics added).

Forrest believes that his unhappiness lies in his lack of material success (as he perceives "success"), and in the failure of those around him to appreciate his brilliance, drive and dedication. Yet from the Buddhist and Stoic perspectives, none of these "problems" is capable of determining Forrest's happiness or unhappiness. Rather, it is Forrest's *perspective* on these issues that creates the feelings he has. For example, most people struggling to pay their mortgage would probably have little sympathy for Forrest's complaint that he doesn't have a house on the Cape and another in the Hamptons!

In this regard, the Thai Buddhist master, Ajahn Chah, presents a telling anecdote that illustrates this concept of perspective. He recounts how one day, a hog farmer came to see him, complaining bitterly about his business. The price of hog feed was up! The price of pork was down! "I'm losing my shirt!" the man railed. Ajahn Chah listened calmly to the farmer's complaints, then replied, "Don't feel too sorry for yourself, sir. If you were a pig, then you'd have good reason to feel sorry for yourself. When the price of pork is high, the pigs are slaughtered. When . . . [it] is low, the pigs are still slaughtered. The pigs really have something to complain about." (from *Everything Arises, Everything Falls Away*, p. 26).

Finally, the Stoics would again point out that eliciting the praise and appreciation of others is simply not within our control. So why torment ourselves about these things? Marcus Aurelius might very well say to Forrest,

> "You say, people [do not] admire the sharpness of your wits—so be it: but . . . [you can] show those qualities which are altogether in your power: sincerity, gravity, endurance of labor . . . contentment with your portion and with few things, benevolence, [and] frankness." (slightly modified from *Meditations*).

*   *   *

Chapter 4

THE COMMON BOND OF HUMANITY

Judaism

"Love your fellow as yourself."

—Leviticus 19:18

"Beloved is the human being, since he was created in God's image . . ."

—Talmud, Pirke Avot 3:18

"Whoever destroys a soul, it is considered as if he destroyed an entire world. And whoever saves a life, it is considered as if he saved an entire world."

—Jerusalem Talmud, Sanhedrin 4:1 (22a)

". . . we must treat people properly because all people play a role in God's plans; nobody was created for naught, be it a fool, an ignoramus, or even an evil person. They are all part of the Divine Scheme . . ."

—Rabbi Moshe Lieber

"If your enemy is hungry, give him bread to eat."

—Proverbs 25:21

"A person should be more concerned with spiritual than with material matters, but another person's material welfare is his own spiritual concern."

—*Rabbi Israel Salanter*

Buddhism

". . . all sentient beings, including humans, are endowed with Buddha-nature . . . [defined as] the potential for full awakening, or as the essential perfection of each sentient being . . ."

—B. Allen Wallace

"[Buddhism is] not based on a metaphysical or doctrinal position, but on an existential experience common to all humanity—the experience of suffering."

—Ajahn Sumedho

"Compassion is natural to every one of us, but because we have deep, very self-centered habits, we need to cultivate [compassion] by contemplating the suffering of . . . [others]."

—Chagdud Tulku

"Having cultivated a selfless, loving concern for another person's well-being, the next step is to develop this toward others, eventually embracing all sentient beings . . . this is the foundation for great compassion."

—B. Allan Wallace

Stoicism

"If a person could be persuaded of this principle as he ought, that we are all originally descended from God, and that he is the Father of all on earth and in heaven . . . [one] would never think of himself meanly or ignobly."

—Epictetus

"You carry God about with you, poor wretch, and you know nothing of Him."

—Epictetus

"All things are woven together and the common bond is sacred . . . for there is one Universe out of all, one God through all, one substance and one law, one common Reason of all intelligent creatures, and one truth . . ."

—Marcus Aurelius, Meditations

". . . consider the connection of all things in the universe and their relation to one another. For in a manner all things are implicated with one another, and all in this way are friendly to one another . . ."

—Marcus Aurelius, Meditations

Pete's Prejudice

Pete was a retired businessman, married for over thirty years to Kate. Although Pete had many social acquaintances and "buddies," and was regarded as "a decent guy" by most who knew him, he had no close friends in whom he could confide. Kate—a retired school teacher—had always been concerned by some of Pete's attitudes toward "strangers." As she put it to one of her close friends, "Pete almost always seems suspicious of anyone who doesn't fit his idea of "our kind of people." Sometimes, it's a little scary, and he gets really paranoid about some of our immigrant neighbors." Recently, a family from Colombia had moved in to the house next to Pete and Kate. Pete complained to Kate that, "These people are always doing shady things. You know, up late at night, with cars always pulling up to the house. They're probably doing drug deals—you know those damn Colombians." Pete had been brought up in a residential institution for abandoned and orphaned children and did not know his biological parents. Apparently, he had "a rough time" as a child, and alluded in very vague terms to some kind of emotional or physical abuse, while in the orphanage. Pete had overcome his early adversity, however, and had managed to earn a master's degree in business administration. He had worked for over thirty years as the business manager of a small manufacturing firm, and had put aside a decent "nest egg" for retirement. Despite the couple's material comfort, Pete often felt he had "gotten the short end of the stick." He complained that the country was being run by "foreigners who don't really understand America" and who "are out to screw anybody who made it on his own." Although Pete had been active in some community activities, such as his local church, he had become increasingly isolated since retiring two years ago. He spent much of his time, as Kate put it, "writing rants to the local newspaper", usually regarding "outside agitators" and "people who don't belong here", whom he blamed for many of the country's economic woes. "These people—they slip across the border dripping wet, and then they expect a free hand-out from the folks who paid their dues." When his Colombian neighbor—a young medical technician named Alejandro—tried to introduce himself one day, Pete simply scowled and went back in the house.

Later, when Pete learned that Alejandro's wife was chronically ill, he experienced a brief pang of regret at having been unfriendly. However, he made no attempt to "reach out" to Alejandro and his family. Feeling ashamed of her husband's behavior, Kate went over to the neighbors' house with a homemade cake, and welcomed Alejandro and his wife, Rosa, to the neighborhood.

The Jewish Perspective

The Talmud tells us, "Beloved is the human being, since he was created in God's image . . ." (Pirke Avot 3:18). This teaching is clearly not confined to how Jews should view other Jews. As Rabbi Michael Hattin observes,

> "The Torah was the first and only code to promulgate the revolutionary idea that all human beings, irrespective of race, color or creed, were descended from a single man and woman who were fashioned in the 'Divine Image.' This implied, by extension, that all members of humanity were related to each other by a common bond of blood and destiny, and that all were equal in the sight of their benevolent Creator . . . All people have a right to be treated with respect and honor by virtue of their 'Divine Image,' the basic, elemental dignity that is a function not of man's fancy but of God's fiat. *Jew or non-Jew, heathen or Monotheist, all were created in 'God's image.'* (italics added, Parashat Kedoshim, *Love Your Fellow as Yourself*; vbm-torah.org/archive/intparsha/vayikra/30-60kedoshim.doc)

It's clear that, for whatever reasons, Pete has been unable or unwilling to embrace this point of view. Perhaps his apparent "abuse" as a child in the residential setting left Pete unable to trust others, particularly those he considers "alien." And yet, he *was* able to find a wife and sustain a marriage over thirty years, so we may presume that Pete is capable of a certain degree of trust.

The Judaic principle that, "Whoever destroys a soul, it is considered as if he destroyed an entire world. And whoever saves a life, it is considered as if he saved an entire world," has been held up to critical scrutiny in recent years. It seems that the movie, "Schindler's List" quoted this teaching, prompting some to argue that the Talmud advocates only the saving of *Jewish* lives, not *all* lives. Here, we need to introduce a point not discussed in Chapter 1: *there are actually two closely related versions of the Talmud.* It is true that in the *Babylonian* Talmud (Sanhedrin 37a), the phrases "a soul from Israel" and "a life from Israel" are used. However, in the *Jerusalem* Talmud (Sanhedrin 4:1 22a), there is no mention of "Israel" or any reference to saving only "Jewish" lives. The teaching is as I have quoted it in full. Furthermore, as Rabbi Gil Student has pointed out, the more universal formulation appears in three other places in the rabbinical literature (see http://www.angelfire.com/mt/talmud/schindler.html

One outgrowth of this Judaic view of humanity is the belief that we should treat "strangers" with decency and respect. Thus, in the book of Exodus (22:20), we are told, 'You shall not wrong a stranger, nor oppress him; for you were strangers in the land of Egypt' (Ex. 22:20). Then, twenty verses later we are told: 'Also you shall not oppress a stranger; for you know the heart of a stranger, seeing you were strangers in the land of Egypt' (Ex. 23:9). Why are we told essentially the same thing twice, in so short a space? Rabbi Danny Burkeman suggests the following explanation:

"The repetition of the commandment suggests two things to us. First of all it makes it clear that this is an important instruction, one that requires reiteration to make sure that it is not ignored. God was unwilling to take the chance that this commandment would be lost in a Torah portion, which contains fifty-three separate commandments. But on a secondary level, the need to repeat this commandment might reveal something about the way we are often inclined to treat the stranger. Maybe our 'natural' reaction is to oppress the stranger or to wrong him, and so we need to be told twice that this is inappropriate and against God's will." [*www.wls.org.uk/Download-document/433-Parashat-Mishpatim*]

As a psychiatrist, I find the phrase, ". . . *you know the heart of a stranger . . .*" especially important. It suggests that the experience of the Jewish people should have created a certain kind of *empathy* for the "stranger in a strange land"—to borrow from Robert Heinlein's 1961 science fiction novel, which may have alluded to the passage in Exodus. Yet, as Pete's story demonstrates, developing such empathy is not easy—and not just for those raised in residential settings, without loving parents. Developing empathy for others is a struggle for all of us, and especially so when the "other" seems alien, foreign, or "not one of us." And so, as Rabbi Burkeman suggests, we need to be reminded that treating strangers with respect and dignity is our moral obligation.

The Torah gives us a wonderful example of how we are to treat the "stranger", through the personage of Abraham—the first patriarch of the Jewish people, and the father of the three "Abrahamic" faiths (Judaism, Christianity, and Islam). We are told, for example, that Abraham would actually *seek out* strangers and offer them a meal!—an example followed by Pete's wife, Kate, in our introductory vignette. Thus, we find, in Genesis 18, the story of how Abraham was sitting at the entrance of his tent and noticed three strangers. He ran towards them and invited them to come to his home, where he washed their feet and provided them with bread.

Abraham's love of humanity is even more dramatically demonstrated when he "bargains" with God Himself, over the destruction of the evil cities of Sodom and Gomorra (Genesis 18:25). In effect, Abraham pleads for the lives of perfect strangers, whom God seeks to destroy, asking the Lord, "Shall not the Judge of all the earth do justly?" This is all the more remarkable, given that the people of Sodom were known for having banned acts of charity and hospitality! To this day, showing hospitality, especially to strangers, is among the most sacred of obligations in Judaism. (There are exceptions, of course; for example, if the "stranger" is known to be a dangerous or disreputable person). This obligation is much more than showing "good manners", in the style of Emily Post! Rather, hospitality and respect toward "the other" is predicated on the Jewish belief (as Rabbi Dovid Rosenfeld puts it) that ". . . God created everything and everyone so that something good and beneficial will come from each of them."

The Buddhist Perspective

In the Buddhist world-view, every event, every creature, every human being is linked in some fundamental and inexorable way. This is so, not merely because all events spring from an endless, causal chain of antecedent events. We are also linked to our fellow creatures through what Buddhists call *samsara*—" . . . the cycle of birth, aging, sickness, and death, [and] the cycle of being propelled from one life to another by the force of one's

own mental distortions and the actions conditioned by them."
(Wallace, p. 40). In Tibetan Buddhism, it is believed not only
that we have all had countless previous lives, but that all beings
". . . at some time throughout countless lifetimes . . . have shown
us the kindness of parents, given us a body, protected us, [and]
enabled us to survive . . ." (Tulku, p. 35). In essence, when you
meet a stranger, you can never be sure that he or she was not your
parent in a previous life!

Now, this is a difficult and perhaps unnecessary teaching,
for our purposes, but it has very practical consequences for how
we are to behave toward one another. For example, Buddhist
teachers may instruct us to "see every being as your mother",
as a way of *counteracting our anger* toward someone. (Chagdud
Tulku, for example, asserts clearly that ". . . all beings, at one
time or another through countless lifetimes, have been our own
mother . . ." (Tulku, p. 111)

Following this advice may be quite a difficult feat, if your
boss is chewing you out at work—and, as Prof. Stephen Prothero
has observed, it may not help someone who had a very troubled
relationship with his mother! Nevertheless, the underlying
principle is worthy of our respect. For Buddhists, not only are we
all in the same boat; we are all, in an important sense, *in the same
web of creation.* Shantideva urged us to see ourselves and others
as being "limbs of the same body," as a means of developing
empathy for others (Wallace, p. 159).

To put the matter in terms of what we have called "the flourishing
life",

> "Everyone wants to be happy, but happiness cannot
> be achieved in isolation. The happiness of one
> depends upon the happiness of all and the happiness
> of all depends upon the happiness of one. This is

because all life is interdependent. In order to be
happy, one needs to cultivate wholesome attitudes
towards others in society and towards all sentient
beings."   (http://www.buddhanet.net/e-learning/
buddhism/bs-s15.htm (Buddha Dharma Education
Association).

As B. Alan Wallace has noted, the basis for this universal wish
for happiness is our "Buddha-nature." He goes on to note that

"We must initially take the existence of Buddha-nature on
faith, but it can be aroused . . . in our daily lives. How? One
crucial element is the cultivation of great compassion, which is
grounded in the understanding that all sentient beings are alike
in terms of their essential nature." (*Tibetan Buddhism from the
Ground Up*, p. 151)

But if this is so obvious, how is it that so many of us think
and behave like Pete? Why do so many insult, disparage and
disrespect those of other faiths, races, or national origins? Again,
Wallace provides a partial answer:

"The false sense of "I" . . . exerts a strong influence
on our other mental functions and on the course of
our lives . . . The false notion of selfhood gives rise to
a feeling of separateness from everyone else, and from
this follows the affliction of attachment . . . Pride is a
mental factor based on a distorted view of the self . . .
with a sense of conceit and superiority . . . Pride,
while originating from ignorance, also reinforces the
false sense of ego, exalting it as superior to other egos."
(*Tibetan Buddhism from the Ground Up*, p. 54).

Yes, the combination of attachment, ignorance and conceit
sounds all too familiar, and Pete seems to be an example of this

toxic brew. Yet if we denigrate Pete and reduce him to a kind of "Archie Bunker" stereotype, *we are engaging in precisely what Buddhism counsels against*: drawing sharp lines of difference and separation among our fellow human beings! Whatever Pete's failings, we can find a long chain of causal explanations for them. No, this does not *excuse* his behavior, but it helps *explain* it—and it helps us see Pete as part of the very fallible community of human beings to which we all belong.

This brings us back to the most fundamental Buddhist justification for including everyone in the human community, and for treating everyone with respect and dignity: in the words of Ajahn Sumedho, abbot of the Amaravati Buddhist Centre: "[Buddhism is] not based on a metaphysical or doctrinal position, but on an existential experience common to all humanity—the experience of suffering." (http://sharanam.tumblr.com/post/5639926098/is-buddhism-a-religion)

To be sure, as Pete's case shows us, it is not easy to appreciate this common bond, or to act on it in our daily lives. Indeed, as Chagdud Tulku observes, "Compassion is natural to every one of us, but because we have deep, very self-centered habits, we need to cultivate [compassion] by contemplating the suffering of . . . [others]. Chagdud Tulku goes on to say that,

> ". . . equanimity . . . [is] an attitude of equality toward all beings. If we can live free of prejudice or bias, without making a division in our minds between friends and enemies, then we have grasped the essence of existence and planted the seeds of our own and others' happiness and freedom . . . through the practice of equanimity, we develop a noble attitude of compassion for all beings without distinction . . . realizing that all beings, equally, want happiness. Nobody wants to suffer . . ." (p. 111)

The Stoic Perspective

Stoicism is often identified with a kind of cold, hard logic, or a "stiff upper lip" attitude. But in truth, Stoic philosophy is surprisingly humane—even tender-hearted—in its view of the common bond that unites all human beings. Thus, we began this chapter with the epigram from Marcus Aurelius:

> "All things are woven together and the common bond is sacred . . . for there is one Universe out of all, one God through all, one substance and one law, one common Reason of all intelligent creatures, and one truth . . ."

In the work of the Roman statesman, Cicero (106 BCE-43 BCE), we see the full flowering of the "Natural law" ideal in Stoicism. Cicero, for example, tells us that, ". . . we are all subject to one and the same law of Nature; and, if this . . . is true, we are certainly forbidden by Nature's law to wrong our neighbor." (from *On Obligations*). Clearly, Pete's shunning of his neighbor—while not "wrong" in the legal sense—is still a moral shortcoming, in the Stoic scheme of things. Indeed, for Cicero, ". . . there is a bond of community that links every man in the world with every other . . ." and ". . . this bond is universal in application . . ." (from *On Duties*, III, transl. by Michael Grant). As the classicist Michael Grant summarizes Cicero's views,

> ". . . all human beings, however humble, must count for something, must have some inherent value in themselves . . . [for there is a] spark off divinity [that] supplies an unbreakable bond of kinship between one man and another, irrespective of state, race, or caste, in a universal Brotherhood of Man;

and it is right and necessary that brothers should
receive decent treatment from one another." (from
the Introduction, p. 12, Cicero, *Selected Works*).

The Stoic principle that we all contain a "spark of divinity"
requires a bit more comment. When Epictetus, tells us that
". . . we are all originally descended from God, and . . . he is the
Father of all on earth and in heaven . . ." he sounds strikingly like
the Rabbis of the Talmud! On the other hand, the Stoic idea of
"God" differs considerably from the God of the ancient Hebrews,
and from what most modern monotheists would understand by
the term "God". Most of the Stoics did not conceive of God
as an omniscient, omnipotent being who listens to our prayers
and intercedes directly in human affairs. Rather, the Stoics
typically identified "God" with Nature; with the Universe itself;
and with the underlying *order and reason* that pervades the
Universe. The Stoic "logos" was essentially this same principle
of order and reason, now viewed as *inherent in the rational,
human soul*—knitting together all mankind in the same fabric
of rationality. (We find similar views many centuries later, in the
writings of the philosopher, Baruch Spinoza).

These metaphysical and theological issues need not trouble
us in our appraisal of Pete, of whom the Stoics would have
disapproved heartily! Pete, you will recall, tends to divide the
world into "Us" and "Them." He views strangers or foreigners
with suspicion and contempt, and perhaps with a touch of
paranoia (". . . They're probably doing drug deals—you know
those damn Colombians.") This surely cuts against the grain of
Stoic tolerance and universal brotherhood. As Prof. John Anthony
McGuckin puts it, the Stoic school was

". . . one of the few philosophical movements in
antiquity to speak openly about the equality of all

rational human beings, and the inconsistency of
social distinctions (not least, slavery). Friendship
was highly emphasized as the bond of charity
that underpinned society." (from *The Westminster
Handbook to Patristic Theology*, p. 320)

Pete's suspicious and nearly paranoid attitude toward "the
other" also violates the Stoics' insistence that *we see reality clearly,*
without distortion. Thus, Epictetus says, "Because of our neglect
to study the proper valuation of the phenomena of existence, we
always exaggerate, and represent things to ourselves, greater than
the reality." (XIX).

Finally, Epictetus also observes—quite like our modern
cognitive psychologists—that ". . . by our own preconceived
notions, we distress and torment ourselves." This certainly
applies to Pete's disgruntled resentment, and his feeling that he
has "gotten the short end of the stick." A good Stoic philosopher
would ask, "And what makes you think that *you*, Pete—rather
than your neighbor—are entitled to the "long end" of the stick?
*If you fulfill your duties, you have what belongs to you. And another
person cannot hurt you, unless you allow him to hurt you.*" The
statements in italics were actually made by Epictetus.

Synthesis and Commentary

The concept of "universal brotherhood" (and sisterhood) is a
common element in Judaism, Buddhism, and Stoicism. That
there is a common bond uniting all human beings is also expressed
in many secular philosophies, as President John F. Kennedy
eloquently demonstrated in his June 10, 1963 commencement
address at American University. Kennedy observed that, "Our
most basic common link is that we all inhabit this planet. We all

breathe the same air. We all cherish our children's future. And we are all mortal."

I noted earlier that Pete's apparent "abuse" as a child in the residential setting may have left him unable to trust others, particularly those he considers "alien." There is some research to support this hypothesis. For example, childhood institutionalization may be associated with behavioral problems, as we have learned from studies of children raised in Russian orphanages that provided very little emotional support to the institutionalized children. Some of these children lack the ability to trust others, as they enter adolescence and adulthood.

But, as we emphasize throughout these chapters, the "JuBuSto" tradition stresses the ability of rational human beings to *overcome* these early, sometimes destructive, childhood influences. As James Atlas observed in the May 13, 2012 New York Times, "Self-awareness sets us free." And self-awareness is the very keystone in the arch that joins Judaism, Buddhism and Stoicism. Of course, as each tradition would acknowledge, "self-awareness" does not come easily or naturally to us. It requires practice, discipline and daily effort.

Although the three traditions all reach a similar conclusion regarding the common bond of humanity, they approach it from somewhat different premises. The Judaic tradition begins with the premise that ". . ."Beloved is the human being, since he was created in God's image . . ." (Talmud, *Pirke Avot* 3:18). The divine origin of all mankind—Jews and non-Jews alike—knits all of us into a single tapestry of human dignity. And Hillel's famous formulation of the "Golden Rule"—"Do not do to others what is hateful to you"—applies to *all* persons, regardless of race or religion.

In the Buddhist tradition, there is no clear "deity" in whose image we are all created. However, all of us are said to possess the "Buddha-nature", which is conceived as "the potential for full awakening"; that is, we are all capable of recovering our deepest and most genuine selves. Furthermore—and perhaps of even greater importance—all humanity shares the experience of *dukkha*, or suffering.

Ironically—and sometimes, tragically—we often avoid the suffering of others, even shunning those who are sick or in pain. As Rabbi Michael Leo Samuel observes,

> "Oftentimes loved ones cannot face their moribund parents, family members, and friends when they are suffering. This is a characteristic that human beings share with many species of animals, which will shun a fellow creature that has been wounded or is dying. To become a caregiver, one must make peace with one's own mortality. The person who is languishing in bed could just as easily be you or me at another time of our lives. Would we want to feel as though we are abandoned? Being with a sick person—if nothing else—affirms our common bond of humanity. As caregivers, we must creatively find a way to enable the sick or needy to make it through those dark nights of the soul." (http://rabbimichaelsamuel.com/2009/07/the-book-of-job-as-a-pastoral-parable/)

The Stoic tradition, too, teaches us to have compassion for others, and to treat every human being with respect and dignity. Recalling Pete's animosity toward immigrants and foreigners, it is noteworthy that Cicero—a proudly patrician citizen of Rome—goes out of his way to condemn such attitudes. He writes, in his essay, *On Duties*, that

"... Wrong is ... done by those who ban and eject
foreigners from their cities ... True, non-citizens
are not entitled to the rights of citizens ... but
the exclusion of aliens from the city's amenities is
completely opposed to natural human relations."

Finally, Albert Einstein—a deeply spiritual man, whose
concept of God had affinities with the Stoic *logos*—also appreciated
the common bond that unites all of us. This awakened in him a
profound appreciation of our interdependence, and of the need
to return some of the blessings which have been bestowed upon
us by others. Einstein wrote,

"A hundred times a day I remind myself that my
inner and outer life depend on the labors of other
men, living and dead, and that I must exert myself
in order to give in the measure as I have received and
am still receiving." (Beliefnet.com)

*   *   *

Chapter 5

ETHICAL OBLIGATIONS AND THE FLOURISHING LIFE

Quotations

Judaism

"The reward of a good deed is a good deed; the recompense of sin is sin."

—*Talmud, Pirke Avot 4:2*

"[F]ulfilling a mitzvah [commandment] is a time to feel great joy at your relationship with God."

—Rabbi Alexander Ziskind

"What is the remedy for those whose souls are sick? Let them go to the wise men—who are physicians of the soul—and they will cure their disease by means of the character traits that they shall teach them . . ."

—Maimonides, *Laws Concerning Character Traits*

". . . your mission on earth is not merely to use the material world for your own satisfaction, but to refine and civilize it through virtuous acts."

—Rabbi Menachem Mendel Schneerson

Buddhism

"The Buddhist view is simple: non-virtuous behavior leads to misery: virtuous behavior leads to joy."

—B. Alan Wallace, *Tibetan Buddhism*

"Cultivating good heart throughout daily life; practicing virtue, compassion, equanimity, love and joy—this is the way to enlightenment."

—Chagdud Tulku

"With gladness I rejoice in the ocean of virtue . . . which brings about the well-being of all creatures . . ."

—Shantideva

"Each day, we should do at least one meritorious act . . . don't let a day go by without creating virtue."

—Ajahn Chah

Stoicism

"The Stoics believe that right is the only good."

—Cicero, *On Duties*

"A good character is the only guarantee of everlasting, carefree happiness."

—Seneca, *Letter XXVII* (Campbell, 73)

"What then, must a person do to have what the
Stoics would call a good life? Be virtuous!"
—William Irvine, *A Guide to the Good Life*

"The good for human beings lies in this one
thing alone: for each of us to perfect our moral
character . . ."
—Keith Seddon,
Epictetus' Handbook and the Tablet of Cebes, p. 49

Donald's Debauchery

Donald was a 40-year-old, unmarried writer, who was referred
to a psychotherapist by his family physician. Although Donald
had been highly successful as a well-published author of "crime
novels," he described himself as "kind of a wreck, emotionally." He
complained that he had no close friends, "just people who come
in handy for one reason or another," and that, despite his fame as
a writer, he felt "empty inside . . . like an egg that's been drained of
the yolk." Although he had never been in serious trouble with the
law, Donald had been accused, twice, of plagiarizing material for
his novels. Both cases had been settled out of court, but Donald
acknowledged to his therapist that he had "taken a little here and
there" from two lesser-known authors, without crediting their
work. He joked to his therapist, "You know what T.S. Eliot said,
Doc? 'Mediocre writers borrow. Great writers steal!'" Donald
expressed a philosophy that he described as "part Machiavelli,
part Casanova." He believed that "You have to do unto others
before they do unto you!" and that trying to be ethical and just in
an unethical, unjust world was "a gigantic load of crap." He noted
that, "You have two choices in life, Doc. You can be the little fish
that gets eaten by the shark, or you can be the shark!"

Donald acknowledged that his "philosophy" made it difficult to get along with others, and was often the precipitant of intense arguments with editors and other writers. Donald had never felt emotionally close to anyone, and had never had a serious, intimate relationship with "anybody I really cared about." This was so, despite Donald's impressive string of affairs, which—by his estimate—had included "well over two-hundred women" in the past thirty years. These relationships were essentially brief, sexual encounters, and Donald acknowledged, "I'd be lucky to remember half the names" of the women he had seduced. He also reported spending thousands of dollars a month on his gambling habit, which often kept him "carousing all night and just plain raising hell" in various casinos and bars.

His family physician had treated Donald twice for sexually-transmitted diseases (though Donald was not HIV-positive), which reflected Donald's refusal to practice "safe sex". "I'd rather take my chances and go with my passions, Doc," he stated to his therapist. "I guess I really believe that old saying from the 60s—if it feels good, do it!" Donald had been raised in a household in which his father—a traveling salesman—was mostly absent, and his mother struggled with alcohol abuse. Occasionally, when intoxicated, she would "take the strap to me for no reason at all," Donald told his therapist. He had three older brothers, and described them as ". . . always angling for advantage—like, who was going to be the alpha male in the herd. You had to watch your back or one the guys would put a knife in it, figuratively speaking."

Despite this adverse home environment, Donald had cultivated both an interest in literature, and a considerable talent for writing. A college professor had encouraged him to pursue his literary goals, and after graduation, Donald was accepted into a prestigious writing program. To the dismay of his teachers, however, Donald abandoned any attempt at writing serious fiction or poetry, and vowed to "make a million bucks writing potboilers and sleaze." Though he had succeeded beyond his expectations in this regard, Donald felt ". . . like a fraud—an imposter—masquerading as a writer." He described his mood as "pretty depressed", and on more than one occasion, he had contemplated suicide.

*   *   *

The Jewish Perspective

The Jewish ideal of "the good life" is neither one of austere self-denial, nor of debauched self-indulgence. For the rabbis of the Talmud, the spiritually fulfilled life was one of moderation and reason, grounded in the ethics of God's commandments. As Rabbi Leonard B. Gewirtz has put it in his essay titled, "The Authentic Jew,"

> "The fundamental question of morals turns upon whether man can achieve the good life by pursuing his desires and satisfying them, or whether he must first learn to desire the right kind of ethical happiness . . . Since desires are limitless and man can never satisfy them all, he must learn to discriminate among them and to control them. The basis of discrimination must be that in satisfying his desires, man must not violate the ethical, cultural, and religious demands of his divine soul." (http://www. archive.org/stream/authenticjewandh012856mbp/ authenticjewandh012856mbp_djvu.txt)

In so many obvious ways, Donald has fallen short of this Judaic ideal— and perhaps of his *own* ideal, as well—though he is far from exceptional in our modern, Western culture. Donald sees the world as a "zero-sum game", in which you either devour or get devoured. Anything is justified, if it serves one's personal interests, regardless of the harm it may do others. In stark contrast, as Rabbi Menachem Mendel Schneerson teaches us, the rabbinical tradition sees our mission on earth as ". . . not merely to use the material world for [our] own satisfaction, but to refine and civilize it through virtuous acts." Furthermore, there is a direct connection between a person's *ethical behavior*, and his or her *happiness*. As Rabbi Gewirtz observes,

> "The moral human being is a purpose-seeking animal. He . . . must find life worthwhile and meaningful. He must have a standard that [says] doing one thing is better than doing any other. Unless he has such an overall standard system, life loses its significance. He may move efficiently from task to task, from sale to sale, from one social activity to another; but all this pursuit does not lead to fulfillment. All his busyness seems to lead nowhere; he is moving on a treadmill." (from *The Authentic Jew and his Judaism*)

Indeed, from the Judaic perspective, the person without a moral compass is merely foundering at sea. Like Donald, such an individual often feels ". . . empty inside . . . like an egg that's been drained of the yolk." The code of Machiavelli and Casanova may well bring us transient power or fleeting pleasure—but it can never provide us a sense of inner wholeness or spiritual fulfillment.

But let's be clear: the Judaic tradition does *not* call on us to renounce all pleasure—quite the contrary! The Talmud teaches us that "In the future world, a man will have to give an accounting for every good thing his eyes saw, but of which he did not eat." (Jerusalem Talmud, Kiddushin 4:12). The Talmud is not opposed to moderate sensual indulgence, either. We are told, "Whoever denies himself a little wine is a sinner—and the man who denies himself too many things is a greater sinner." (*Taanit* 11 a, b). At the same time, as Rabbi Gewirtz notes, ". . . man must not violate the ethical, cultural, and religious demands of his divine soul." (from *The Authentic Jew and his Judaism*)

Indeed, in the Judaic world view, following the ethical principles laid down in Jewish law *is itself a source of pleasure and fulfillment. As* Rabbi Alexander Ziskind puts it, fulfilling an ethical obligation ". . . is a time to feel great joy at your relationship with God." Doing the right thing is not experienced as an onerous burden, but as a profound affirmation of our place in the universe. As Rabbi Gewirtz observes, "The scholars and saints in Judaism have always sought the good for its intrinsic value . . . *We do good because it is good to do good.*" (italics added)

Rabbi Dovid Rosenfeld has put the matter in terms of each individual's evolving spirituality and self-integration. He writes that

> ". . . The *mitzvos* [commandments of the Torah] were not given to us in order to earn us reward or free mileage. They are to perfect ourselves, to make ourselves "whole" ("*shalaim*"), in the terminology of Jewish thinkers. By performing all the mitzvos, we become whole and perfected human beings. The Talmud tells us that the Torah contains 248 positive

mitzvos corresponding to the 248 limbs of a person's body (Makkos 23b). (The remaining 365 (out of 613) are negative commandments, correspond to the days of the year.) The message is that each mitzvah perfects our spiritual bodies and our characters in its own unique way." (pirkei-avos-owner@torah.org).

Spiritual growth, in turn, leads to personal happiness. Indeed, many Jewish sages believe it is our *only* means of achieving genuine happiness. We find this expressed in the writings of Rabbi Menachem Mendel Schneerson (1902-94)—known simply as "the Rebbe"—who was the spiritual leader of the Lubavitcher Hasidic community. Regarded by some followers as "the Messiah"—a claim he never voiced himself—the Rebbe saw our ethical commitments in terms of what he called *redemption*. He taught that,

> "Redemption is not necessarily a religious or spiritual matter. Redemption means freedom—freedom from the boundaries that confine the human spirit . . . so we are all looking for redemption, whether we use that word or not . . ." (from *The Meaningful Life*)

And how do we achieve redemption? For the Rebbe, redemption arises from our dedication to *spiritualized living and virtuous action*. Indeed, the Rebbe tells us that ". . . we know true happiness only when we are creatively contributing to our world." Specifically,

> "Because man was created to spiritualize the material world, the only way to reach true happiness is through spiritual growth and achievement. And that means giving to others, loving, and sharing . . . Even the smallest things—a kind word, a dollar to

charity, a few minutes of prayer—are immeasurably significant. We must do anything we can to direct even one ray of light into the darkness." (from *The Meaningful Life*).

The Rebbe is often considered an exemplar of the Jewish "mystical" tradition, though he was well-versed in the physical sciences. In any case, there is little question that the Chassidic tradition is usually contrasted with that of Jewish "rationalism", as represented by the greatest Jewish philosopher of the medieval period, Moshe ben Maimon (ca. 1138-1204). This physician, philosopher and theologian is usually called Maimonides, and is known affectionately as "Rambam" (from the first letters of *Ra*bbi *M*oshe *b*en *M*aimon). For Maimonides, the essence of ethical action lay in the *structure of one's character*. Noble character traits form the foundation for ethical acts, and usually reflect the "mean" between two extremes. Maimonides adopted this perspective from the Greek philosopher, Aristotle (from whom the modern philosopher, Alasdair MacIntyre, has also drawn inspiration). So, for example, the virtue of "courage" represents the mean between the extremes of cowardice and foolhardy bravado. Moral virtue, for Maimonides, was necessary for the well-being of society. But, for Rambam, *a well-developed, moral character was also integral to what we have called "the flourishing life"*. As Weiss and Butterworth put it, for Maimonides,

> ". . . the well-being of society is not the only purpose of morality. Moral virtue also produces *serenity within the individual himself*; a strict moral regimen is needed to quiet the disturbances of the body's impulses." (*Ethical Writings of Maimonides*, p. 4, italics added).

This "inner serenity" is closely related to what the Stoics called *ataraxia* (roughly, "peace of mind"), and is intimately connected with the Greek concept of *eudaimonia*, or "the flourishing life." In her book, *Happiness in Premodern Judaism*, Prof. Hava Tirosh-Samuelson has noted the striking affinity between Aristotle and Maimonides, on what constitutes the "good life":

> "Both [Aristotle and Maimonides] presupposed that the good life springs from the very nature of human beings. Both maintained that the good person must acquire virtues through deliberate, habitual practice of good acts. Both held that the good life requires social interaction, and that such interaction must be guided by the principle of moderation." (p. 193)

For Maimonides, God is fundamentally "a God of moral action" (Guttmann, *The Philosophy of Judaism,* p. 177). And for Maimonides, as for Rabbi Schneerson, *moral action is at the heart of the fulfilled life.* Those who fail to exercise virtue, in Maimonides view, are unable to achieve the good or flourishing life. Specifically, Maimonides understood most mental afflictions as arising from an "imbalance" in one's character traits—for example, veering away from the mean, toward one or the other extreme. If Rambam were to examine Donald's lifestyle, morals, and behavior, he would likely conclude that Donald's sense of inner emptiness reflects the unsettled and turbulent state of his soul, and his apparent contempt for the rights and needs of others.

Sometimes, special help is needed to heal these mentally disturbed individuals—and in this passage, Maimonides could well be describing our modern-day psychologists and psychiatrists:

> "What is the remedy for those whose souls are sick?
> Let them go to the wise men—who are physicians of
> the soul—and they will cure their disease by means
> of the character traits that they shall teach them . . ."
> (from *Laws Concerning Character Traits*)

To be sure: personal equanimity, for Maimonides, was not an end in itself. It was a means ". . . for attaining the contemplative life" and the intellectual freedom we need to become fully human and draw close to God (Weiss and Butterworth, p. 4). Someone like Donald—whose behavior veers from one extreme to another, and who is habitually blown this way and that by his impulses—will be unable to achieve inner serenity, or the contemplative life, unless he begins to re-shape his character. As Rabbi Gewirtz put it, because ". . . desires are limitless and man can never satisfy them all, he must learn to discriminate among them and to control them."

The Buddhist Perspective

As the writer Suvimalee Karunaratna puts it, "The Buddha's prescription for prosperity and happiness . . . is . . . inextricably linked with ethics." (http://www.budsas.org/ebud/ebdha049. htm#ethic). Indeed, you may recall that among the elements of the "Eightfold Path" are *right speech, right conduct,* and *right vocation*—usually considered under the rubric of *sila* (the code of conduct that leads to virtue). The Tibetan Buddhist nun, Thubten Chodron, defines these three elements as ". . . true, kind, and appropriate speech; . . . actions which do not harm others; and . . . obtaining our subsistence—food, clothing and so forth—by non-harmful and honest means." (p. 14).

For Buddhists, a life grounded in ethical action is the foundation for personal well-being and "the good life." As B. Alan Wallace puts it,

> "Establishing a foundation of moral discipline through the cultivation of virtuous behavior brings inner harmony in one's thoughts, emotions, and behavior. One experiences a refreshing serenity that is calm and filled with vitality, a quality that transforms one's relationships with others. Interpersonal strife and conflict are subdued, and a spirit of friendly cooperation arises spontaneously." (B. A. Wallace, p. 93)

It seems clear from Donald's history that his lifestyle is anything but one of "moral discipline." Though he may not acknowledge it, Donald is a slave to his passions and impulses, come what may—even as he exposes himself and others to danger, such as the risk of sexually-transmitted diseases. From the Buddhist perspective, it comes as no surprise that Donald's life is hardly serene and conflict-free. On the contrary, his self-centered, Machiavellian philosophy has led him into "intense arguments" with others—hardly a life of "friendly cooperation."

Thubten Chodron was once asked to define "the essence of the Buddha's teachings." She replied simply, ". . . it is to avoid harming others and to help them as much as possible." She then cited a verse summarizing this teaching:

> Abandon negative action;
> Create perfect virtue;
> Subdue your own mind.
> This is the teaching of the Buddha. (Chodron, p. 13)

Perhaps the most direct way of "creating virtue", according to Buddhist ethics, is by cultivating love and compassion. While this may seem like an altruistic activity, intended to benefit others, it actually has the effect of *enhancing our own lives*, as well. In this sense, love and compassion are integral to what we have called, "the flourishing life." As Chodron puts it:

> "Love and compassion benefit ourselves and others. With [love and compassion], we feel in touch with and connect to all living beings. Feelings of alienation and despair vanish and are replaced with optimism. When we act with . . . [love and compassion], those in our immediate environment benefit . . . Our family feels the difference, as do our colleagues, friends and people we encounter during the day." (Chodron, p. 27). +

Conversely, a failure to achieve what Stephen Batchelor calls "integrity" leaves us less able to pursue our spiritual goals—and thus makes it harder to live a fulfilled life. There is, after all, little point in reciting Buddhist mantras or sitting in meditation if the rest of your life lacks moral integrity. Batchelor writes that,

> "Dharma practice cannot be abstracted from the way we interact with the world . . . if we behave in a way that harms either others or ourselves, the capacity to focus on the [spiritual] task will be weakened. We'll feel disturbed, distracted, uneasy." (*Buddhism Without Beliefs*, p. 45).

In Donald's case, it seems likely that his inner sense of "emptiness" may stem from a dim awareness that his life lacks moral integrity.

In its version of "the good life", Buddhist ethics emphasizes self-control, self-restraint, and avoidance of the "ten unwholesome deeds". These comprise *taking a life, stealing, sexual misconduct, lying, slander, verbal abuse, gossip, avarice, malice,* and *false views* (Wallace, p. 94). Thus, most Buddhist formulations of the good life tend to emphasize *avoidance* of various "bad behaviors". For example, the Buddhist scholar, Prof. Damien Keown, points to a Buddhist text called the "Discourse to Sigala." In this story, the Buddha is giving advice to a young householder named Sigalaka, regarding "the discipline of the noble ones." First, the Buddha describes all those behaviors that destroy a person, and make "the good life" impossible. Some of these will sound very much like elements of Donald's lifestyle:

> "Sleeping late, adultery, hostility, meaninglessness, harmful friends, utter stinginess: These six things destroy a person. Bad friends, bad companions, bad practices—spending time in evil ways, by these, one brings oneself to ruin, in this world and the next. Seduction, gambling, drinking, singing, dancing, sleeping by day, wandering all around untimely . . . These things destroy a person . . ." (translated by John Kelly, Sue Sawyer, and Victoria Yareham). http://www.accesstoinsight.org/tipitaka/dn/dn.31.0.ksw0.html

Then the Buddha describes the life of the truly *good* person, which amounts to the Buddhist description of how one achieves "the good life", for both the individual and humanity:

> "Wise and virtuous, gentle and eloquent, humble and accommodating; such a person attains glory. Energetic, not lazy, not shaken in misfortune,

> flawless in conduct, and intelligent; such a person
> attains glory. A compassionate maker of friends,
> approachable, free from stinginess, a leader, a
> teacher, and diplomat; such a person attains glory.
> Generosity and kind words, conduct for others'
> welfare, impartiality in all things . . . These kind
> dispositions hold the world together, like the
> linchpin of a moving chariot."

This description is quite reminiscent of personal virtues praised in the Talmud, and might be colloquially termed, "the personality traits of a *mensch*." As the translators of the "Discourse to Sigala" note, the ethical life is a "prerequisite" for one's personal and spiritual development, ". . . for a very practical reason; the remorse and guilt that disturb the mind of an immoral person make meditation, and thus progress towards [spiritual] awakening, impossible." In contrast, "One able to maintain the precepts is one who lives a careful, considerate, and mindful existence, most conducive to the development of concentration, wisdom, and ultimately *nibbaana* [*nirvana*, the enlightened state].

The Stoic Perspective

For the Stoics, virtue depends on one's "excellence as a human being", which means how well one "performs the function for which humans were designed . . ." And for what functions were we designed? The Stoics held that humans were designed to live in harmony with nature, and "to be reasonable"—which amount to one and the same activity. (Irvine, *A Guide to the Good Life,* pp. 35-36). Philosopher William Irvine goes on to say that,

". . . if we use our reason, we will further conclude that we were designed to do certain things, that we have certain duties . . . since nature intended us to be social creatures, we have duties to our fellow men. We should, for example, honor our parents, be agreeable to our friends, and be concerned with the interests of our countrymen." (*A Guide to the Good Life*, p. 36).

Cicero, too, views living in harmony with nature as an essentially ethical activity. He writes that

". . . the Stoics' ideal is to live consistently with nature. I suppose what they mean is this: throughout our lives we ought invariably to aim at morally right courses of action . . . there ought never to [be] any question of weighing advantage against right . . ." (from, *On Duties*)

Like the Judaic and Buddhist traditions, Stoic philosophy praises the person who values virtue for its own sake, and asserts that such an individual is truly "happy." Indeed, Seneca insists that, "A good character is the *only* guarantee of everlasting, carefree happiness." (*Letter XXVII*, italics added). That is a remarkable and radical claim, given the widespread, modern view that lasting happiness can be achieved through cosmetic surgery, retirement in Tahiti, or by meeting "that special someone!"

Sometimes, the Stoics speak of *euroia biou*, which Keith Seddon translates as the "good flow of life". Possessing a good character is one essential condition—arguably, *the* essential condition—for this "good flow", according to the Stoics. Thus, Seddon (quoting Epictetus) writes that

> "The good for human beings lies in this one thing alone: for each of us to perfect our moral character, to bring it into harmony with nature, making it 'elevated, free, unhindered, unimpeded, trustworthy, and honorable . . .'" (p. 49, *Epictetus' Handbook*).

In contrast—and here, we are reminded of Donald's risky and promiscuous lifestyle—investing our hopes and energies in transient, sensual pleasures is ultimately fruitless. As Seneca observes,

> ". . . when they're over, pleasures of a depraved nature are apt to carry feelings of dissatisfaction . . . such pleasures are insubstantial and unreliable; even if they don't do one any harm, they're fleeting in character. Look around for some enduring good instead." (*Letter XXVII*)

Some of the Stoics seem to take a very dim view of "pleasure", even in comparison with the Judaic and Buddhist philosophy of moderation and restraint. To be sure, the Stoics were concerned primarily with avoiding ". . . the disagreeable passions of fear and distress . . ." But even "the agreeable passions of desire and pleasure" were regarded with some suspicion—at least, by some of the early Stoics (Seddon, p. 132). Sometimes, a simple human pleasure was regarded as a sign of weak character. One notorious example: the Roman statesman, Cato the Younger (95 BCE-46 BCE) is said to have expressed regret at having kissed his wife in a moment of danger! (from Introduction to Seneca's *Letters from a Stoic*, p. 17).

For such "hard-core" Stoics, it was irrational to regard transient pleasures as "good", because *the only real good is the possession of virtue.* From their point of view, pursuing pleasure carried the risks of neglecting our duties and ". . . treating people unkindly in the pursuit of pleasures . . . thereby living contrary to nature . . . all of which puts happiness and well-being (*eudaimonia*) beyond their grasp." (Seddon, p. 132). We can readily see how these objections to heedless pleasure-seeking apply to Donald, who regards other people as mere extensions of his own needs and desires.

But—is pleasure as such really an *evil*? Or was Cato the Younger making a fetish out of self-discipline? To gain some perspective on the Stoic view, let's recall the Talmudic teaching that, "In the future world, a man will have to give an accounting for every good thing his eyes saw, but of which he did not eat." Indeed, in the Jewish mystical tradition of the *Chassidim,* the point is made even more forcefully. For example, the Baal Shem Tov (Rabbi Yisroel ben Eliezer, 1698-1760) taught that "Pleasures are manifestations of God's love." (Beliefnet). In comparison, the early Stoics may seem like a bunch of cranky kill-joys! Even the usually temperate Seneca sometimes comes off sounding rather "puritanical", at least in this letter (#51) to his friend, Lucilius:

> "We should toughen our minds, and remove them far from the allurements of pleasure. A single winter relaxed Hannibal's fiber; his pampering in Campania took the vigor out of that hero who had triumphed over Alpine snows. He conquered with his weapons, but was conquered by his vices. We too have a war to wage, a type of warfare in which there is allowed no rest or furlough. To be conquered, in the first place, are pleasures, which, as you see, have carried off even the sternest characters." (http://en.wikisource. org/wiki/Moral_letters_to_Lucilius/Letter_51)

Actually—compared with Cato and the earlier Stoics—we see some "softening" of the Stoic world-view in later figures, like Seneca and Marcus Aurelius. Seneca, for example, disparaged "so-called pleasures" when "they go beyond a certain limit", at which point they "are but punishments." (Letter LXXXIII). It is not clear that Seneca condemned more moderate forms of enjoyment, so long as they were consistent with Stoic ethics in general. `

Finally, it must be acknowledged that, while the Stoics did not want to "kill joy", their concept of "joy" was highly idealistic and elevated. Thus, Marcus Aurelius tells us,

> ". . . it is my joy if I keep my governing self intact,
> not turning my back on any human being . . . but
> seeing everything with kind eyes, welcoming and
> employing each occasion according to its merits."
> (from *Meditations*, p. 58, translated by A.S.L.
> Farquharson)

Synthesis and Commentary

As Wallace points out, in the Buddhist tradition, "Loving kindness . . . traditionally starts with oneself, and then proceeds . . . to an attitude of loving kindness toward all sentient beings . . ." (*Tibetan Buddhism from the Ground Up*, p. 119). It seems clear that Donald does not practice loving kindness toward himself; at least, we see no evidence of this in his feeling like "a fraud" and "an imposter." Perhaps on some level, he knows that his "eat or be eaten" philosophy and self-centered actions are unworthy of him—or of any human being. Unable to respect and love himself, it is not surprising he cannot extend these feelings to others. Here, we are again reminded of Hillel's famous questions, "If I am not for myself, who will be for me . . . [but] if I am for myself alone, what am I?"

Of course, we can appreciate the "bad hand" that Donald was dealt as a child. Certainly, any psychotherapist would quickly make the connection between Donald's present behavior and his past privations; for example, his "mostly absent" father; his physically abusive mother; and his scheming, untrustworthy brothers, always "angling for advantage." All these disadvantages are reasons for us to have compassion for Donald, and not condemn him as a human being. Otherwise, we have not learned the lessons of the very traditions we are examining! Nevertheless, the sages of Judaism, Buddhism, and Stoicism would still hold Donald *responsible* for his actions, attitudes, and choices—and all would agree that he is capable of finding a new and better path for himself, if he puts his mind to it.

Ironically, it is Donald's unwillingness to live a morally responsible life that is depriving him of real happiness. In this sense, William Irvine speaks of Stoicism as ". . . a paradoxical recipe for happiness." (p. 35). The paradox is that when we cease to focus relentlessly on being "happy", and, instead, tend to our moral responsibilities, we wind up . . . well, happy! More precisely, we wind up with *eudaimonia*—the flourishing of life.

In our modern, Judeo-Christian culture, we often think of moral actions as *obligations*, perhaps with the implicit expectation of *punishment,* if we fail to carry out some duty. But the JuBuSto tradition emphasizes that it is by living ethical lives—indeed, *only* by living ethical lives—that we actually achieve genuine happiness and become fully human. This is not the transient pleasure of brief, sensual indulgence; it is the enduring sense of fulfillment that comes from attaining the "flourishing life" (*eudaimonia*). For the Rabbis of the Talmud, the Stoics of ancient Greece and Rome; and the sages of Mahayana Buddhism, the fulfilled life is not that of the libertine, but of the person guided by *reason and virtue.*

*   *   *

Chapter 6

DESIRES AND ATTACHMENTS

Judaism

"No man departs from this world with half his cravings satisfied. When he has attained a hundred, he desires two hundred."

—*Midrash Rabbah, Koheles 1:34 and 3:12*

"Rabbi Elazar HaKappar said: Jealousy, lust and the [pursuit of] honor remove a person from the world."

—Pirke Avot 4:28

"Since desires are limitless and man can never satisfy them all, he must learn to discriminate among them and to control them."

—Rabbi Leonard B. Gewirtz
(from *The Authentic Jew and his Judaism*)

"Worldly desires are like sunbeams in a dark room."

—Nahman of Bratslav

Buddhism

"The loss of wealth in itself is not the source of suffering, only attachment to having it."

—Chagdud Tulku

"The extraordinary suffering is the suffering that arises from what we call *upadana*, grasping on to things. This is like having an injection with a syringe filled with poison."

—Ajahn Chah, Living Dhamma p. 36

"Renunciation is not getting rid of the things of this world, but accepting that they pass away."

—*Aitken Roshi*

Stoicism

"Because you are given a less honorable place at the table, you begin to get angry at your host . . . [and] at the man himself who was preferred above you. Madman! What difference does it make on what part of the couch you recline?"

—Seneca, "On Anger"

". . . in no case does what is praised become better or worse . . . Does an emerald become worse than it was, if it be not praised?"

—Marcus Aurelius, Meditations

"Now death and life, good report and evil report, pain and pleasure, wealth and poverty, these all befall men, good and bad alike, equally, and are themselves neither right nor wrong; they are therefore neither good nor ill."

—Marcus Aurelius, Meditations

Annie's Attachments

Annie was a single, 32-year-old business woman who entered therapy with the complaint that, "No matter how successful I am, I never seem to find any real peace or satisfaction." She had graduated with honors from a prestigious business school, earning a master's degree, and soon started her own software company. Although the business had grown considerably over the years, Annie acknowledged that, "It never seems like enough. I always feel like we should be taking in more money, expanding, out-distancing the competition." Annie lived alone in a posh condominium, and led a life of "partying and schmoozing", as she put it. Although she saw herself as "married some day, maybe with a kid," Annie acknowledged that it was hard for her to "get close to anybody." Typically, with both men and women, Annie would feel either jealous or competitive, and wind up quarreling with the person. She felt that those in her social circle ". . . never really say anything good about me" nor did they pay sufficient attention to her needs. As Annie put it, "It's like, I have to beg for a simple, goddamn compliment!" She also admitted being "pretty thin-skinned" and alluded to becoming "furious" with some of her friends when they offered any criticism.

Annie spent much of her free time "hanging out in swanky clubs" or going to singles' bars. Although she prided herself on her appearance, she had put on ten pounds in the past year, "Maybe because when I get a little down in the dumps, I treat myself to rich foods and sweets." Annie also described her penchant for "buying stuff I don't really need, just because it looks great in my condo." Recently, she had purchased a rare painting for more than $20,000, ". . . not because I'm really into art, but just to impress my house guests. And I guess it really irks me if I think they have a nicer place than I have." Annie admitted that she entertained fantasies of ". . . making enough money so that I don't have to worry about buying things I really want." When her therapist asked, "But did you really *want* that painting?" Annie shrugged and replied, "I guess when you put it that way, maybe not. But I want to have the *power* to buy whatever I want, whenever I want it!" She acknowledged that she sometimes went on "shopping binges" that cost several thousand dollars, and that she was "hooked on nice clothing and perfume." She then added, "But, it's like, I buy five or six things and then I get tired of them, and I just go out looking for more stuff."

Annie also described her long-standing habit of taking on new work assignments ". . . even when we are backed up", simply because "I feel like if I don't run at full speed, I'll never get off the tread-mill." When her therapist observed that, "Unless you step off the treadmill, it doesn't matter how fast you run," Annie began to weep softly, and said with some bitterness, "Don't you think I *know* that? I wish I knew *how* to step off it!"

The Perspective of Judaism

The sages of the Talmud knew very well the seductive—even the addictive—quality of "attachments". We often think of attachments in material terms, as we see in Annie's compulsive need to shop for clothing and perfume. But we humans find all kinds of ways to create attachments—whether to objects, emotions, activities, relationships, or even ideas. We often speak of the "craving" associated with such attachments, which, in extreme cases, becomes a kind of addictive process. And often, it seems there is no end to our lusts, desires, and cravings. The great medieval sage, Maimonides, put it as clearly as anyone, more than eight centuries ago:

> "All the difficulties and troubles we meet [in daily life] are due to the desire for superfluous things . . . the more we desire to have the superfluous, the more we meet with difficulties." (from *The Guide for the Perplexed*, book 3, chapter 12).

Maimonides went on to link the insatiable desire for "stuff" with jealousy toward those who have more:

> "When the soul becomes accustomed to superfluous things, it acquires a strong habit . . . [and] this desire can be limitless. But things that are truly necessary are few in number . . . What is superfluous is endless. For example, you desire to have your vessels made of silver, but golden vessels are still better . . . Those who are ignorant and perverse in their thought are constantly in trouble and pain because they cannot get as much of superfluous things as someone else possesses." (from *The Guide for the Perplexed*, Book 3, chapter 12).

And, as Rabbi I.M. Bunim affirms, little has changed from the time of Maimonides to our own:

> "Our tradition knows only too well that a human being is capable of insatiable desires. No sooner is one craving satisfied than two new ones take its place. Says the Midrash, "No man departs from the world with even half of his desires attained . . . If he has a

> hundred, he wants to make two hundred of them; if
> he has two hundred, he wants to make four hundred
> of them." . . . How truly it describes people of our time
> and every time: for as a person begins to increase his
> earnings, he tends to raise his standard of living, only
> to find soon that he needs and yearns for still more
> money . . . [and] to continue up the ladder of luxury
> and social prestige." (*Ethics from Sinai*, p. 193)

Maimonides represents the "rationalist" strain of rabbinical thinking. In the Jewish mystical tradition, excessive craving or desire is understood as part of the "evil impulse" or *yetzer hara*. The evil impulse, in turn, is often personified as, "the Evil One," in some Hasidic writing—a figure usually called "Satan" in the Biblical literature. (The topic of Satan would take us far afield; however, Rabbi Louis Jacobs' comment is very instructive: ". . . Satan is the personification of both a demonic power outside man and the urge to do evil in the human psyche."—*Concise Companion to the Jewish Religion*). The Evil One is seen as a kind of "trickster", luring us with the promise of fulfilling our desires, but ultimately disappointing us. In the words of the Hasidic master, Nahman of Bratslav,

> "[The Evil One] fools the world, tricking everyone
> into following him. All men think that his hand
> contains what they desire. But in the end, when he
> opens his hand, there is nothing in it. No worldly
> desire is ever fulfilled. Worldly desires are like
> sunbeams in a dark room. They may seem solid,
> but the person who tries to grasp a sunbeam finds
> nothing in his hand. The same is true of all worldly
> desires." [from Besserman, *The Way of the Jewish
> Mystics*, p. 155, translated by Aryeh Kaplan]

In Annie's plaintive acknowledgement, "No matter how successful I am, I never seem to find any real peace or satisfaction," perhaps we hear this sense of finding "nothing" in the Evil One's hand. In this regard, we find an interesting teaching from the Talmudic sage, Rabbi Elazar HaKapar: "Envy, desire, and pursuit of honor remove a person from the world." [Pirke Avot 4:21].

What does this mean, and how does it relate to Annie's "attachments"? In discussing this teaching, Rabbi Raymond Beyda notes that

> "Envy is a trait that focuses a person on the traits and the possessions of others. When one is constantly looking outward at what others possess, one always finds someone who has more than he or she has and the result is a sense of dissatisfaction with one's lot in life. Desire works in a similar fashion to push one to chase after whatever is new in the physical realm or even merely to work hard to accumulate wealth in spite of the fact that one has enough to live comfortably . . . One who seeks honor is chasing something that one will never have enough of to satisfy. Pursuit of these traits is like drinking salt water. It does not quench a thirst; rather, the more you drink the thirstier you become. Since there is nothing that can quiet these false needs, the one who chases these unachievable goals . . . cannot find satisfaction in this world." (rbeyda@torah.org)

Recall that Annie tells her therapist that, "It never seems like enough. I always feel like we should be taking in more money, expanding, out-distancing the competition." She also relates that, with both men and women, she winds up feeling "either jealous or competitive." Consumed by such ceaseless and fruitless

striving, Annie is indeed "removed" from the world—she is
unable to enjoy the social, intellectual, spiritual or artistic riches
of the world, because she is caught up in her own little world of
craving and attachment. At the same time, it's important to note,
in the words of Rabbi Jack Bemporad, that

> "Judaism sees nothing wrong with ambition in and
> of itself or the desire to achieve something in one's
> life for oneself and those we love. It simply condemns
> the self-centered ambition realized at the expense of
> others." (from *The Inner Journey,* 2007.)

Similarly, Annie alludes to wanting the "power" to "buy
whatever I want, whenever I want it!" But what sort of "power"
is that? It's certainly not the power to live a more fulfilled life,
or to gain control over one's health or emotional well-being. As
Maimonides observed,

> ". . . one who has . . . [great riches] has not thereby
> obtained control over anything that could be an
> essential addition to his being, but has only obtained
> something illusory or deceptive." (from *The Guide
> for the Perplexed*, Book 3, chapter 12).

And yet—there is a "flip-side" to this matter of attachment,
and Maimonides was well aware of it. He recognized that there is
a risk of erring *too far* on the side of self-denial and asceticism:

> "Maybe a person would say, 'Since jealousy, desire
> and honor and the like are bad ways and they take
> people out of the world, I will separate myself from
> them completely and to the extreme until I will not
> eat meat nor drink wine, and not get married, and

not live in a nice home, and not wear nice clothing, but only sackcloth and harsh wool I will wear like those idolaters.' This, too, is a bad way to be, and it is forbidden to walk on this path . . . Therefore, the sages commanded that one should not deny himself anything that the Torah itself did not prohibit, and that he should not deny himself that which is permitted to him with oaths and vows. The sages said the following: "The Torah has not forbidden enough things without you looking for further prohibitions?" Similarly, those who fast all the time are not considered to be following the good way and the Sages forbade a person from afflicting himself by fasting."—Maimonides, *The Laws of Behavior,* Chapter 3 [http://www.jewishvirtuallibrary.org/jsource/Judaism/Desire.html]

It might even be argued that someone prone to such extreme self-denial and self-affliction is no less "attached" to these habits than the one, like Annie, who clings to material pleasures and self-aggrandizement.

The Perspective of Buddhism

In chapter 1, we dealt with the concept of *tanha,* which we defined as, "blind demandingness." We noted that it is not unfortunate events themselves that make us unhappy, but rather, as E.A. Burtt put it,

". . . the blind demandingness (*tanha*) in our nature, which leads us to ask of the universe . . . more than

it is ready or even able to give." (from *The Teachings
of the Compassionate Buddha*).

This "demandingness" often takes the form of intense cravings,
desires, and attachments—which, if frustrated, leave us feeling
unhappy, angry or cheated. Thus, in the *Dhammapada*—a famous
text from the Theravadan Buddhist tradition—we are taught, "A
man who gives way to pleasure will be swept away by craving and
his thoughts will make him suffer, like waves." (v. 339)

Many people who are "swept away" by their cravings seem to
be avoiding the larger issues in their life. For example, Annie—by
clinging to her shopping sprees, petty jealousies, and extravagant
life-style—seems to be hiding from her own loneliness and sense
of futility. No wonder she breaks down and becomes tearful
when confronted by her therapist! One of the most frequently
avoided issues, for most of us, is the ever-present shadow of our
own mortality. After all, as Annie's life attests, it's much easier to
occupy ourselves with power-struggles at work, over-indulgence
in eating and drinking, and expensive shopping sprees than to
confront the fact that all of us, all too soon, will cease to exist. As
B. Alan Wallace puts it,

> "As long as we ignore our inevitable death and
> the absolute uncertainty of the time when it will
> occur, we feel free to indulge in pointless talk and
> in being preoccupied with food, drink, and other
> sensual pleasures. Strong craving arises for material
> acquisitions and prestige, and we become infuriated
> when we encounter obstacles. Thus, the ignorance,
> pride, jealousy and other afflictions this denial
> causes dominate our minds relentlessly; and these
> incite behavior that brings us more misery both in
> the near and far future." (p. 13)

In Zen Buddhism, the ideal goal is "annihilation of attachment"; but, as Jacob Yuroh Teshima observes, this really means ". . . annihilating superficial thoughts and passions" in order to allow the emergence of "the internal true self" (*Zen Buddhism and Hasidism*, pp. 98-99). Indeed, it's ironic that the more we avoid the issue of our own mortality and focus on the pursuit of power and pleasure, the more "deadened" to life we become, and the less connected we are to our "true selves." As the great teacher of Zen Buddhism, Alan W. Watts, puts it, our grasping, clutching, life-style becomes

> ". . . a quenching of thirst with salt water, a pursuit of goals which simply require the pursuit of other goals, a clutching of objects which the swift course of time renders as insubstantial as mist. The very one who pursues . . . sees that his grasp upon the world is his strangle-hold about his own neck, the hold which is depriving him of the very life he so longs to attain." (*The Way of Zen*, p. 66).

So—how do we break free of this strangle-hold? Paradoxically, focusing too intently on becoming "enlightened" or reaching "nirvana" can itself become another form of attachment, as Watts points out. Thus, in the Pure Land School of Buddhism, it is held that ". . . all efforts to become a Buddha are merely the false pride of the ego." (Watts, p. 68). So—how do we break out of this bind?

One way, as Chagdud Tulku teaches us, is by realizing how fleeting our attachments are. In his words,

> "We can lessen attachment by contemplating impermanence. It is certain that whatever we're attached to will either change or be lost. A person

may die or go away, a friend may become an enemy,
a thief may steal our money. Even our body, to which
we're most attached, will be gone one day. Knowing
this not only helps to reduce our attachment, but
[also] gives us a greater appreciation of what we
have while we have it . . . *Driven by desire, we don't
appreciate the preciousness of what we already have."*
(pp. 8-9, italics added)

But just as we saw in the Jewish tradition, Buddhist
sages teach that we can "overshoot" the dangers of sensual
pleasure-seeking, and catapult ourselves directly into a *more subtle
form of attachment.* No less a personage than Shakyamuni—the
Buddha himself!—puts it this way:

"Let me tell you about the middle path. Dressing
in rough and dirty garments, letting your hair grow
matted, abstaining from eating any meat or fish, does
not cleanse the one who is deluded. Mortifying the
flesh through excessive hardship does not lead to a
triumph over the senses. All self-inflicted suffering is
useless as long as the feeling of self is dominant. You
should lose your involvement with yourself and then
eat and drink naturally, according to the needs of
your body. Attachment to your appetites—whether
you deprive or indulge them—can lead to slavery,
but satisfying the needs of daily life is not wrong.
Indeed, to keep a body in good health is a duty, for
otherwise the mind will not stay strong and clear."
Discourses II (http://viewonbuddhism.org/)

This "middle path" of Buddhism has much in common with
Aristotle's doctrine of the "golden mean", which so influenced

Maimonides—and, as we shall see, with Stoic values as well. Finally, we should not confuse the Buddhist idea of non-attachment with the *avoidance of pleasure*. Once, when the Tibetan Buddhist nun, Thubten Chodron, was asked, "Wouldn't life be boring without attachment?" she gave a wise and nuanced reply:

> "No. In fact it's attachment that makes us restless and prevents us from enjoying things. For example, suppose we're attached to chocolate cake. Even while we're eating it, we're not tasting it and enjoying it completely. We're usually either criticizing ourselves for eating something fattening, comparing the taste of this chocolate cake to other cakes we've eaten in the past, or planning how to get another piece. In any case, we're not really experiencing the chocolate cake in the present. On the other hand, without attachment, we can think clearly about whether we want to eat the cake, and if we decide to, we can eat it peacefully, tasting and enjoying every bite without craving for more or being dissatisfied because it isn't as good as we expected. As we diminish our attachment, life becomes more interesting because we're able to open up to what's happening in each moment."
> (Thubten Chodron, *Buddhism for Beginners*, p. 88)

The Stoic Perspective

Philosopher William Irvine has put the Stoic view of "attachment and desire" very succinctly:

> "We humans are unhappy in large part because we are insatiable; after working hard to get what

we want, we routinely lose interest in the object of
our desire. Rather than feeling satisfied, we feel a
bit bored and . . . go on to form new, even grander
desires." (*A Guide to the Good Life*, p. 66).

We are reminded, in this description, of Annie's comment,
". . . it's like, I buy five or six things and then I get tired of them, and
I just go out looking for more stuff." Since, for the Stoics, the only
real "good" in life is *virtue*, it is axiomatic that acquiring material
possessions, wealth, honor, prestige, and influence are merely
illusory goods. And when these supposed goods become false
gods, we sacrifice the very core of our human dignity. Annie's case
reflects this teaching, as when she notes, "No matter how successful
I am, I never seem to find any real peace or satisfaction."

In Christian theology—a huge topic beyond the scope of
our inquiry—we often hear the statement, "The Lord giveth,
and the Lord taketh away." The essence of the message is that we
should not allow ourselves to become too "attached" to worldly
possessions, wealth, or even our loved ones, since God is the
ultimate "owner" of everything. Actually, the quote is a variant
translation of Job's words, in the "Old Testament" (*Tanakh*),
when Job says, "Naked I came from my mother's womb, and
naked shall I return; the Lord gave, and the Lord has taken
away; blessed be the name of the Lord." (*Oxford Annotated Bible*,
Revised Standard Version). Now, while the Stoics are not known
for their belief in "God" in the Judeo-Christian sense, some
Stoics come remarkably close to paraphrasing Job's statement. In
his *Handbook*, for example, Epictetus voices the Stoic view of
"attachment"—regarding not only material possessions, but also
the most cherished relationships in our lives:

"Never say of anything, 'I have lost it,' but rather, 'I
have given it back.' Has your child died? It has been

given back. Has your wife died? She has been given back. Has your land been taken from you? Well, that too has been given back . . . What concern is it of yours by whose hand the Giver asks for its return? For the time that these things are given to you, take care of them as things that belong to another, just as travelers do at an inn." (from K. Seddon, p. 65).

Well, to be sure, these Stoic admonitions may strike us as "cold" or callous—after all, how could any parent view the death of a child as merely the return of a "thing"? How could any husband or wife lose a spouse and view such an immense tragedy as simply "giving back" that which belongs to God, "the Giver"? Most mental health professionals would rightly argue that anyone who undergoes so profound a loss needs time to grieve and mourn—and this is often a process that goes on for many months, or even years. The grief of bereavement is, indeed, a natural and healthy part of healing—and not something that can merely be rationalized away, through *any* kind of philosophy!

And so, we may not be able to follow Epictetus in his cool and stringent form of "non-attachment"—but we may still learn from his admonitions. For example, we may have a prized family heirloom that is lost in a house fire; or worse, we may suffer the loss of house and home, owing to some natural disaster. We can take heart from the Stoic concept that nothing in the world truly "belongs" to us—and that, in a profound sense, we are all "borrowers" and guests in this world, much like travelers at the inn.

Some people of deep faith seem to understand this. For example, during Hurricane Katrina, ". . . a 30-foot wall of water from Lake Ponchartrain slammed into the small community surrounding Hartzell Mt. Zion [United Methodist Church], soaking all the homes and leaving the people with nothing," according to Global Ministries News Archives. The report notes that,

> "Donald Y. Archie, lay leader of the church, walked inside his water-soaked church for the first time this Sunday. He said he had been putting off looking inside. When he came back outside he said, "*The Lord giveth and the Lord taketh away, blessed be the name of the Lord.*" With tears in his eyes, he said, "We'll come back." (K.L. Gilbert).

The Stoics would have considerable admiration for Mr. Archie. Yet for most of us, it's probably easier to grasp the Stoic view of non-attachment as applied to more mundane matters, of the sort described in Annie's case. Here is how Keith Seddon summarizes the Stoic view:

> ". . . for the uneducated person, external things [*ta ektos*] are everything (or almost always so.) Such people live their lives in pursuit of them, wishing to have possession and power over them; they measure their status against what and how many [possessions] they have, and they believe that their well-being is determined by the success of this enterprise. When well-being eludes them (as, according to the Stoic teaching, it must often or always do), they immediately believe that this results from some deficiency in the external things, over which they struggle to maintain power; or from a specific lack of this item or that, which now they pursue, in the belief that in acquiring it, they will also secure well-being. It is this desire for external things that

the [student of Stoicism] is trying to extinguish . . ."
(Seddon, pp. 70-71).

In Annie's case, her almost compulsive pursuit of material gain, power, and social status is surely deadening her spiritual growth and thwarting her desire for "well-being". The flourishing life may not demand the level of detachment that Epictetus advocates, but it *does* require that we cease our worship of "external things." Indeed, the Stoics believed that,

> ". . . one cannot have two objectives at the same
> time: to secure external things and to keep one's
> moral character (*prohairesis*) in accordance with
> nature: these aims are not compatible . . . To attempt
> to perfect one's moral character requires abandoning
> one's belief that external things can be truly good
> and can have genuine value." (Seddon, p. 72).

Synthesis and Commentary

The great writer and lexicographer, Dr. Samuel Johnson (1709-84) said, "Every man is rich or poor according to the proportion between his desires and his enjoyments." Indeed, we have explored this critical "ratio" in two case vignettes. In chapter 3, we discussed Forrest's preoccupation with wealth and success. In this chapter, we broadened our discussion to the topic of "desires and attachments" in general, and explored their impact in the case of Annie. In truth, "wealth and success" are merely two common forms of attachment. Many people are also unduly "attached" to a particular ideology, religion, political view, or personal relationship. All these forms of attachment have in common *an "over-valuation" of transient things*, such that they become a source of stress and emotional imbalance. Under such undue influence, we become slaves to our desires rather than masters of our lives. Perhaps this is what the poet, William Wordsworth, had in mind, in these lines from his sonnet:

> The world is too much with us; late and soon,
> Getting and spending, we lay waste our powers:
> Little we see in Nature that is ours . . .

The German mystic, Meister Eckhart (ca 1260-1327), put it even more succinctly: "To be full of things is to be empty of God."

Psychoanalysts have examined the phenomenon of "greed" and noted that,

> ". . . For some, greed is experienced as a constant hunger, a feeling of being empty and alone. This type of patient can be aggressive or resentful in the way they feel and act. They are determined to take what they feel is rightly theirs. Other such patients are much more conflicted about their greedy [fantasies] and striving." (R. Waska, <u>Am J Psychoanal.</u> 2004 Sep;64(3):253-6).

Indeed, Waska's term, "psychic hunger" aptly describes those, like Annie, who seem almost insatiable in their need to be "fed" with various material things—or to feed their egos with success, power, and conquest. Almost inevitably, such individuals find that they are still "hungry", and wind up feeling empty and alone, much like Annie. It's no wonder that friendship and intimacy come hard to these unfortunate souls. Most emotionally healthy people can sense that bottomless "hunger", and instinctively back away from it. After all, who wants to serve as a mere object to be "devoured", in order to feed another person's ego? That kind of relationship is what the Jewish philosopher, Martin Buber, called an "I-It, rather than an "I-Thou" relationship.

All three of our spiritual traditions—to varying degrees, and from somewhat differing perspectives—agree on the need to avoid undue "attachments." The Judaic perspective holds that, "Envy, desire, and pursuit of honor remove a person from the world." We might understand this as removing the person from the genuine enjoyment of life, and from one's real purpose as a human being: to live an ethical life, and to make the world a better place. Thus, rabbinical tradition speaks of *tikkun olam*—the responsibility of "repairing the world." One can't do that and also be fixated on wealth, status, and power.

The Buddhist tradition emphasizes how excessive attachment represents a refusal to come to grips with the transient nature of all things—including our own lives. As Chagdud Tulku teaches us, the contemplation of impermanence ". . . not only helps to reduce our attachment, but [also] gives us a greater appreciation of what we have while we have it." The Stoics, too, see attachment and the "desire for external things" as a kind of fool's errand—one that inevitably leaves us feeling empty, dissatisfied, and incapable of achieving *euroia biou*—a "good flow of life." We must choose: either we live the life of "getting and spending", or the life of reason in accordance with Nature. We cannot have it both ways.

*   *   *

Chapter 7

IMPERMANENCE AND MORTALITY

Judaism

"The day is short, the task is great, the workers are lazy, and reward is great, and the Master of the house is insistent."

—Pirke Avot 2:20

"Burial shrouds are made without pockets because only good deeds and acts of kindness belong to someone after death; everything else remains behind." (Treasury, p. 133).

—Rabbi Moshe Lieber

". . . repent one day before your death."

—Pirke Avot 2:15

"Death is the haven of life, and old age the ship which enters the port."

—Talmud (Lankevich, p. 47)

"*Tzedakah* [Righteousness] can save from death."

—Talmud, Bava Batra 10a

Buddhism

"If it doesn't break today, it will break tomorrow. If it doesn't break tomorrow, it will break the day after tomorrow. Things that are subject to being broken are not where you should be placing your trust."
—Ajahn Chah, Everything Arises, pp. 17-18

"'Here shall I dwell in the season of rains, and here in winter and summer'; thus thinks the fool, but he does not think of death . . ."
—Dhammapada 20:286-289 (Mascaro, p. 76).

"Death does not happen only to others. Nor when I want it to."
—Stephen Batchelor, Buddhism Without Beliefs, p. 30

"Neither father, sons nor one's relations can stop the King of Death. When he comes with all his power, a man's relations cannot save him. A man who is virtuous and wise understands the meaning of this, and swiftly strives with all his might to clear a path to Nirvana."
—Dhammapada 20:288-289 (Mascaro, p. 76).

Stoicism

"Since it is possible that you may depart from life this very moment, regard every act and thought accordingly."
—Marcus Aurelius

[T]he one who lives longest and the one who will
die soonest lose just the same."

—Marcus Aurelius

"[A] life is never incomplete if it is an honorable
one. At whatever point you leave life, if you leave it
in the right way, it is a whole."

—Seneca, Letter LXXVII

"As it is with a play, so it is with life—what matters
is not how long the acting lasts, but how good it is."

—Seneca, Letter LXXVII

Daniel's Denial

Daniel was a 48-year-old, married, father of two, who sought the
advice of his family physician because of recent "panic attacks"
and "nightmares." He came to the doctor's office requesting
"Something I can take for these damn anxiety spells," but, after
ruling out any underlying medical illnesses, his doctor advised
Daniel to see a psychiatrist. Reluctantly, and with some anger,
Daniel agreed to do so.

He told the psychiatrist that, for the past two months,
he had been "waking up in a cold sweat, from these terrible
nightmares . . . my heart pounds, I have trouble breathing—it
feels like I'm choking!" Daniel denied experiencing any such
attacks in the day time, but acknowledged that "I'm always keyed
up, always on edge lately." He was baffled as to the cause of his
anxiety and nightmares, but noted, "The marriage isn't going
so hot, and, now that both boys are off at college, the house is
like a damn funeral parlor. I don't know, Doc, maybe I'm just
bored." The psychiatrist thought the "funeral parlor" description

was an unusual choice of words, and began to explore Daniel's nightmares. "They're always a little different each time, but one keeps repeating. I'm in my car, driving through the country on a sunny day, when suddenly, there's this awful smell in the car—like rotten meat or fish. I look over at the passenger's seat, and I see myself as a teenager, just sitting there smiling. But the smell keeps getting stronger, and when I look over at my younger self again, my face has started to rot away, like in those zombie movies. I've had this damn dream, like, three times in the last week!"

The psychiatrist began to explore Daniel's developmental and early adult history, as well as his current marital difficulties. Daniel's mother had died when he was only 7, and he had been raised by an alcoholic father. As an adolescent, Daniel had been "kind of a dare-devil", and had actually been stopped by the police at age 17 for "reckless endangerment" while driving his father's car. Daniel smirked while relating this, saying, "A friend and I were playing chicken in our cars, but I was the one who got stopped by the cops!"

Despite his stormy teenage years, Daniel had managed to graduate from college and obtain a business degree. He married in his late 20s, and eventually became a successful stockbroker. "I made a fortune because I was willing to take chances," he told the psychiatrist, but then added. "Unfortunately, I lost a lot of money when the economy tanked." Daniel described his marriage as "OK, but kind of 'blah." Cindy kind of minds her business and I mind mine." But as the session went on, Daniel acknowledged that in the past six months, he had been having an affair with a young assistant in his office. "I'm not proud of it, Doc. But, you know—I just feel great around this girl—like I'm back in my college days!" He described how close he was to his two sons, aged 19 and 21, and how much he missed them both. "They're great guys. It's like, when they left for college, they sucked the oxygen out of the house."

The referral note from Daniel's family doctor noted that, "Despite my frequent warnings, Daniel has not been very compliant with my medical care over the years. He has significant hypertension, but has thus far refused to follow appropriate dietary and weight guidelines, and he is unwilling to take medication. He tends to drink more than is good for him, and only recently gave up smoking after I told him he was a set-up for lung cancer." When confronted with these issues, Daniel remarked, "Hey, Doc, I've got an iron constitution! They're gonna have to shoot me, because otherwise, I'll live to be a hundred." Although Daniel denied any obsessive thoughts or ideas, he acknowledged that, "I am kinda superstitious. Like, I won't do a big online options trade unless I've pitched a penny into this beer mug I keep on my desk. If I miss, I don't do the trade." Daniel acknowledged a "hell of a lot of stress" in his line of work, and had promised himself a vacation many times over the past ten years. "I never take it, though. It's just lost business. And besides, I tell myself there's always next year."

Later in the course of psychotherapy, the psychiatrist began gently to explore Daniel's fantasies and fears about death. When asked, "What do you imagine when you think about your own death?" Daniel replied, "I try not to go there, Doc. To me, death is pain and suffering. That's how my mom died—it was awful, having to watch that. And it's all meaningless—like, what's the point in building a life, if it all gets destroyed in the end anyway? It just isn't fair!"

The Perspective of Judaism

As Rabbi Jack Bemporad has noted (personal communication, 6/18/12), the central ethical precept in Judaism is *the sanctification of life*. Indeed, the traditional pronouncement whenever Jews raise a glass of wine in celebration is, *"L'chaim!"*—"To life!" The sages of the Talmud were well aware of how fleeting life is, and how hard it is to do all the things we want and need to do, within our brief life spans. Thus, Rabbi Tarfon taught, "The day is short, the task is great, the workers are lazy . . . [the] reward is great, and the Master of the house is insistent." (Pirke Avot, 2.20).

The "task", for the Rabbis, was the study of Torah—but we may understand this teaching as applying to any great spiritual quest we may undertake. The "lazy workers" are most of us ordinary human beings; the "Master of the House", not surprisingly, is God; and the "reward" is the spiritual merit we can accrue, if—and *only* if—we make good use of our mortal days! Thus, as Rabbi Moshe Lieber teaches us, "Life is a fleeting opportunity to gather [spiritual] treasure; once the time is up, [one] can no longer earn anything." (Treasury, p. 124).

And so, unlike Daniel—who seems to believe there is "always next year" and that he will "live to be a hundred"—the Talmudic sages knew that no one can assume that life will continue another year, or even another hour! As Rabbi Moshe Lieber explains, the admonition to ". . . repent one day before your death" may be understood in this way:

> "Does one ever know when he will die? Rather, he must always assume that today is the last day of his life and not push off his repentance. Hence, he will spend all his life in perpetual self-improvement." (Lieber, p. 106).

Rabbi Lieber also notes an alternative translation of this passage—as "Repent *even* one day before your death," adding: "By repenting even on his dying day, [one] can redefine his entire life . . ." (Lieber, p. 107). In short, it is never too late to turn over the proverbial new leaf.

As we'll see in our "Synthesis" section, there are clear indications that Daniel's insouciant and cocky attitude toward death is not all that it seems—for now, let's just say that the man doth protest too much! But one thing is clear: he is badly neglecting his own health, on the dubious theory that he's got "an iron constitution." The Jewish view of such self-neglect is very disapproving. The Talmud puts it clearly: "A person is not permitted to harm himself (or herself)". The principle in question is known as *shemirat haguf* ("taking care of the body"). Daniel's refusal to adhere to his doctor's advice is a form of self-harm (and perhaps also Daniel's unconscious way of "tempting death"—more on this later). In the rabbinical view, such behavior is contrary not only to good health, but to also to our moral obligation as human beings. As Maimonides puts it,

> "Since preserving the body's health and strength is among the ways of the Lord—for to attain understanding and knowledge is impossible when one is sick—a man needs to keep away from things that destroy the body, and to accustom himself to things that make him healthy and vigorous." (*Laws Concerning Character Traits*, chapter 4; cited in Weiss and Butterworth 1975, 36).

But notwithstanding the immense value Judaism places on the spiritually-fulfilled life, the Jewish world-view does not see death as something unnatural, or as a thing to be feared or loathed. (For somewhat different reasons, this is also true in Buddhism and Stoicism, as we shall see). Rather, the Talmud says that, "Death is the haven of life, and old age the ship which enters the port." Even in the Hebrew Bible, we find that death is viewed as a regular occurrence in the "seasons" of life. As we read in Ecclesiastes, "A season is set for everything, a time for every experience under heaven; a time for being born, and a time for dying." (7:2). Although he was not a traditionally-observant Jew, Albert Einstein had these words as he approached his own death: "It is tasteless to prolong life artificially. I have done my share, it is time to go. I will do it elegantly." (http://www.catholiceducation. org/articles/catholic_stories/cs0388.htm)

Similarly, in the Jewish confessional prayer known as the "Viduy"—usually recited as one's death approaches—we find a serene acceptance of God's will:

> *"I acknowledge before You, O Lord my G-d and G-d of*
> *my fathers, that my life and death are in Your hands.*
> *May it be Your will to heal me. But if death is my lot,*
> *then I accept it from Your hand with love."*

Indeed, the great German-Jewish philosopher, Hermann Cohen (1842-1918) writes,

> "It is characteristic of the psychology of the Jew that
> he does not fear death . . . By the prayers of their
> survivors, we observe the memory of our dead in
> the pious hope that their souls will have been united
> with those of our patriarchs and matriarchs . . .
> Death is peace, and the grave is the house of
> eternity . . . the virtuous path of peace leads to this
> eternity . . ." (from "Peace and Death", in S. Noveck,
> *Contemporary Jewish Thought*, pp. 172-73).

Of course, for those who do not believe in the immortality of the soul, or in an afterlife, Cohen's point of view may be of little consolation. But Judaism offers us a way of overcoming death, without our having to endorse the idea of a heavenly afterlife—a path that has to do not with how we die, but with how we *live*.

The Talmud teaches us that, "*Tzedakah tahtzeel memavet.*" (Bava Batra 10a, and also Proverbs 10:2). That is, "*Tzedakah* (Righteousness) can save from death." But what does this statement really mean? First, we need to understand a bit about the term "tzedakah", a term often translated as "charity." But this is misleading. Our English word, "charity" is derived from the Latin *caritas*, meaning "from the heart". On the other hand, as Rabbi Joseph Telushkin points out, the word *tzedakah* is derived from *tzedek*, meaning "justice". So, *tzedakah* is much more than just dropping a dollar into the slot of the Salvation Army kettle. As Telushkin says, ". . . one who gives *tzedakah is* acting justly, while one who doesn't is acting unjustly . . ." Indeed, he continues, ". . . Jewish law regards withholding *tzedakah* as not only ugly but also *illegal*." (Telushkin, 2000, p. 74, italics added).

Fine—but in what sense does *tzedakah* "save from death"? Rabbi Stephen Pearce helps us understand the meaning of this by relating a tale from writer Hugh Nissenson's story, "The Elephant and My Jewish Problem." The narrator, Jacob, describes his childhood home as follows:

> "We always had a guest on Friday nights, someone poorer than we, who had no place to celebrate the Sabbath. It was a religious obligation. On Friday afternoons, my father took an hour off from work to wander the streets of the neighborhood, looking for a Jewish beggar or a starving Hebrew scholar who slept on the benches of some *shul* . . . Very often on a particularly cold night, my father invited them to remain with us. They slept on the floor, covered by a woolen blanket. Their snoring made it impossible for me to sleep. "'Papa,' I'd complain.
>
> "'Shhh!' he'd tell me. 'Remember. "*Tzedakah tahtzeel memavet.*" [Righteousness] saves from

death.' He quoted the proverb (10:2) from the Bible in Hebrew, and I shut up."

Even on a Sabbath when Jacob's dying mother was hospitalized, an indigent houseguest was present at the Sabbath table. Later, Jacob couldn't sleep because of the beggar's snoring. His father called to him:

"What's the matter?"

"I can't sleep."

"Neither could I."

"'But I feel much better now."

"'Do you? Why?'

"Because Mama will get well."

"How can you be so sure?"

"You said so yourself."

"Did I? When?"

"You said that [righteousness] saves from death."

"What's that got to do with Mama?"

"Everything."

He suddenly raised his voice. "Is that what you think a *mitzvah* [commandment] is? A bribe offered the Almighty?"

"But you said so. You said that '[righteousness] saves from death.'"

With that the beggar groaned in his sleep.

"No, not Mama," (my father said in a hoarse voice). "*Him.*" (pointing to the beggar)."

In short, Judaism teaches us that death may be overcome *through acts of righteousness and loving-kindness.* To be sure, it is not our *own* death that we overcome. Rather, we may save the life of one less fortunate than ourselves, and thereby, *contribute to the life of the entire community.* (Recall the Talmudic maxim, "Whoever destroys a soul, it is considered as if he destroyed

an entire world. And whoever saves a life, it is considered as if
he saved an entire world.") No, this is not exactly an ascent to
heavenly paradise—but it is one way each of us can transcend
death. As Rabbi Abraham Joshua Heschel eloquently put it,
shortly after having survived a serious heart attack,

> "Life's ultimate meaning remains obscure unless it
> is reflected upon in the face of death . . . [Judaism's]
> central concern is not how to escape death but
> rather, how to sanctify life." (from "Reflections on
> Death", quoted in Sherwin and Cohen, *Creating an
> Ethical Jewish Life*, p. 141)

The Buddhist Perspective

As we have noted in earlier chapters, Buddhism tells us that there
are two roots of unhappiness in human existence: there is *dukha*,
which is the inevitable unhappiness that comes with human
suffering, frailty, disease, loss of loved ones, and of course, death.
Then there is *tanha*, which is translated as "blind demandingness".
The reader will recall that *tanha* is that part of our nature ". . .
which leads us to ask of the universe . . . more than it is ready
or even able to give." (Burtt, p. 28). For example, asking God or
Fate or the Universe never to take away those we love is a form
of *tanha*. So is the demand that we live forever, or enjoy a long,
healthy life free of illness or pain. (Of course, we can *strive* for
such a life, but to *demand* it is to ask more of universe than it
can possibly give!). Parting with these forms of attachment is by
no means easy—but when we do so, we often find that the bitter
taste of our grief begins to dissipate.

   As we have noted on several occasions, the Buddhist way
of decreasing attachment is by contemplating *impermanence*

(anicca). This is surely true of material objects and possessions. As Ajahn Chah bluntly puts it, "If it doesn't break today, it will break tomorrow. If it doesn't break tomorrow, it will break the day after tomorrow. Things that are subject to being broken are not where you should be placing your trust."

The habit of "grasping onto things" is called *upadana*, in Sanskrit and Pali. But Ajahn Chah's teaching also applies to our *lives themselves*! Ultimately, Buddhism encourages us to become less attached even to what is most dear to us—*our own existence*. Here is what Ajahn Chah has to say on this:

> "Suppose you were sick and had to go into the hospital. Most people think, "Please don't let me die, I want to get better." That is wrong thinking, [and] it will lead to suffering. You have to think to yourself, "If I recover, I recover, if I die, I die." This is right thinking, because you can't ultimately control conditions. If you think like this, whether you die or recover, you can't go wrong, you don't have to worry. Wanting to get better at all costs, and afraid of the thought of dying . . . this is the mind which doesn't understand conditions . . ." (from *Living Dharma*, p. 37).

I must confess, this is a little too much "right thinking" for me! I doubt that many of us will reach—or would even want to reach—Ajahn Chah's level of placid acceptance of both life *and* death. This attitude strikes me as a kind of indifference to the sacred nature of life. And yet, Ajahn Chah's teaching is not very far from the sentiment we found in the *viduy* prayer in Judaism; i.e., when we say to God, "*May it be Your will to heal me. But if death is my lot, then I accept it from Your hand with love.*"

Now, Buddhism holds that we will undergo countless other lives in the eternal cycle of birth, death and re-birth, known as *samsara*. Nevertheless, the person who blithely believes—like Daniel—that he will "live to be a hundred" is counted a fool, in Buddhist teachings. In the *Dhammapada*—an ancient text traditionally ascribed to the Buddha himself—we find this description of the "self-satisfied" and oblivious individual:

> "'Here shall I dwell in the season of rains, and here in winter and summer'; thus thinks the fool, but he does not think of death . . . For death carries away the man whose mind is self-satisfied . . . a man who is virtuous and wise understands the meaning of this, and swiftly strives with all his might to clear a path to Nirvana."—Dhammapada 20:286-289 (Mascaro, p. 76).

And again, in the *Dhammapada*, we find this very stark representation of human frailty:

> "Consider this body! A painted puppet with jointed limbs, sometimes suffering and covered with ulcers, full of imaginings, never permanent . . . a house of bones is this body, bones covered with flesh and with blood. Pride and hypocrisy dwell in this house and also old age and death . . . but the virtue of the good never grows old, and thus they can teach the good to those who are good."—*Dhammapada* 11:147, 150-151 (Mascaro, p. 56).

Notice that both passages from the Dhammapada point to the "way out" of self-satisfied attachment to our bodies and our lives: *the path of virtuous action.* In order to "clear a path to Nirvana", we must behave morally in this life, and help others to do so, as well ("teach the good to those who are good"). We are here reminded of the Jewish teaching discussed above: *Righteousness overcomes death.*

Like Judaism, Buddhism demands that we confront the reality of death forthrightly—a difficult spiritual task that Daniel (like most of us) has scrupulously avoided! But Steven Batchelor teaches us that the contemplation of death is not some morbid obsession in the manner of an Edgar Allen Poe story; rather, contemplating death is a way of *recalibrating our life.* As Batchelor puts it,

> ". . . we may discover that death meditation is not a morbid exercise at all. Only when we lose the use of something taken for granted . . . are we jolted into a recognition of its value . . . In taking life for granted, we likewise fail to notice it . . . [but] by meditating on death, we paradoxically become conscious of life. How extraordinary it is to be here at all. Awareness of death can jolt us awake to the sensuality of existence. Breath is no longer a routine inhalation of air but a quivering intake of life. The eye is quickened to the play of light and shade and color, the ear to the intricate medley of sound . . . over time, such meditation penetrates our primary sense of being in the world . . . [and] helps us value more deeply our relationships with others . . . it evokes the poignancy implicit in the [transience] of all things." (pp. 32-33, *Buddhism Without Beliefs*).

The Stoic Perspective

The Stoics tend to be rather unsentimental and, well—downright *stoic,* when it comes to death. They see death as simply one of many natural processes, as Marcus Aurelius writes:

> ". . . wait for [death] as one of the operations of nature. As you now wait for the time when the child shall come out of your wife's womb, so be ready for the time when your soul shall fall out of this envelope . . ." (*Meditations*)

Marcus softens the blow of death just a bit, by pointing out that, after all, we are really simply being transformed by death into our "proper parts".

> "That which has died falls not out of the universe. If it stays here, it also changes here, and is dissolved into its proper parts, which are elements of the universe and of yourself. And these too change, and they murmur not."—Marcus Aurelius (G. Long, p. 168).

Marcus's words are reminiscent of those found in Genesis 3:19, when God says to Adam, "*From dust thou art, and unto dust thou shalt* return."

The underlying premise of the Stoic view of death is summarized by Seneca, in his letter IX (*Letters from a Stoic*). He writes that the enlightened person has a habit of ". . . not regarding as valuable anything that is capable of being taken away." (Note the affinity with the Buddhist concepts of non-attachment *(alobha)* and impermanence). The Stoic sage is one who is able to ". . . [carry] his valuables intact through cities burnt to ashes, for he is contented with himself." (However, Seneca softens this position considerably in acknowledging the importance of companionship; i.e., the enlightened person ". . . is self-content, and yet he would refuse to live if he had to live without any human company at all . . ."—perhaps a somewhat contradictory or ambivalent position on Seneca's part).

Seneca teaches us many things about growing old and dealing with the almost inevitable decline in our bodily function in old age. He knew whereof he spoke: Seneca had suffered for many years with severe attacks of asthma—yet note his rather puckish and self-deprecating sense of humor:

> "Put me in the list of the decrepit, the ones on the very brink! However, I congratulate myself . . . on the fact that my old age has not . . . brought any deterioration in my spirit, conscious as I am of the deterioration in my constitution." (Letter XXVI)

He notes that ". . . [my] spirit is full of life," and adds: ". . . . what cause can there be for complaint, after all, in anything that was always bound to come to an end, fading gradually away?" (Letter XXVI).

Like many Stoic philosophers, Seneca argued that we ought to prepare ourselves for the inevitable end of life. Quoting the philosopher Epicurus, Seneca argues that we ought to "rehearse death." (Ironically, it seems that Roman physicians at that time referred to asthma as "rehearsing death.") But Seneca does not have in mind some macabre ritual involving mock funeral ceremonies! Rather, to "rehearse death" is to "rehearse [one's] freedom." What does Seneca mean by this odd claim? He goes on to say that ". . . there is but one chain holding us in fetters, and that is our love of life."

So is Seneca saying that our freedom lies in *letting go of our love of life*? Is he advocating the sort of "death-loving" attitude seen in some modern-day extremist sects? No—that goes too far for the ever-moderate and sensible Seneca. But he does say this:

> ". . . there is no need to cast this love [of life] out altogether, but it does need to be lessened somewhat, so that nothing may stand in the way of our being prepared to do what we must do at some time or other."

In essence, Seneca seems to be saying, "By all means, love life—but not so obsessively that you will be bitter about parting with it." We see in this something very similar to the Buddhist concepts of non-attachment (*alobha*) and impermanence (*anicca*).

Seneca puts the matter in terms of accepting the natural and inevitable:

> "Wouldn't you think a man a prize fool if he burst into tears because he didn't live a thousand years ago? A man is as much a fool for shedding tears because he isn't going to be alive a thousand years from now. There's no difference between the one and the other—you didn't exist and you won't exist—you've no concern with either period . . . You will go the way that all things go. What is strange about that? That is the law to which you were born; it was the lot of your father, your mother, your ancestors and all who came before you as it will be of all who come after you . . . Every journey has its end." (from Letter LXXVII).

Seneca even goes so far as to advocate not merely accepting death, but *willing it* as something that is necessary. He writes that the wise person ". . . escapes necessity because he wills what necessity is going to force on him." This idea is similar to what the philosopher, Friedrich Nietzsche, many centuries later, would call, "*amor fati*"—basically, "loving fate." This may seem a very strange, if not perverse, idea to our modern temperament. Yet the late Steve Jobs reflected a bit of Seneca's philosophy, when he said, in his 2005 Stanford commencement speech,

> "No one wants to die. Even people who want to go to heaven don't want to die to get there. And yet death is the destination we all share. No one has ever escaped it. And that is as it should be, because *Death is very likely the single best invention of Life*. It is Life's change agent. It clears out the old to make way for the new. Right now the new is you, but someday not too long from now, you will gradually become the old and be cleared away . . ." (italics added)

But while the Stoics urge calm acceptance of the inevitable, they are *not* advocating gloominess, passivity or hopelessness, in the face of our own mortality. Seneca tells us of his struggle with severe, life-long asthma attacks, and says, "Even as I fought for breath . . . I never ceased to find comfort in cheerful and courageous reflections . . ." (Letter LV). Finally, Seneca gives us a kind of summing up of his views on life and death: "The man whom you should admire and imitate is the one who finds it a joy to live, and in spite of that, is not reluctant to die."

Perhaps the most bracing and noble Stoic discourse on impermanence, aging and death is Cicero's (106 B.C.-43 B.C.) essay on "Old Age." In terms reminiscent of Dylan Thomas's poem, "Do Not Go Gentle into that Good Night," Cicero writes:

"The course of life is fixed, and nature admits of its being run but in one way, and only once; and to each part of our life there is something specially seasonable; so that . . . the high spirit of youth, the soberness of maturer years, and the ripe wisdom of old age—all have a certain natural advantage which should be secured in its proper season. [Nevertheless] . . . we must stand up against old age and make up for its drawbacks by taking pains . . . We must look after our health, use moderate exercise, take just enough food and drink to recruit, but not to overload, our strength. Nor is it the body alone that must be supported, but the intellect and soul much more. For they are like lamps: unless you feed them with oil, they too go out from old age . . . The fact is that old age is respectable just as long as it asserts itself, maintains its proper rights, and is not enslaved to anyone." (Cicero, *On Old Age*; translated by E. S. Shuckburgh)

Synthesis and Commentary

The stark reality of death is absolute and universal; it makes no exception for the learned, the wealthy, the handsome, or the privileged. As Shakespeare, in his play, *Cymbeline*, put it:

> *Golden lads and girls all must,*
> *As chimney-sweepers, come to dust.*
> *The scepter, learning, physic must*
> *All follow this and come to dust.*
> (Shakespeare, *Cymbeline, IV.II*)

And yet, few of us care to dwell on the idea of our own death, and there is a sense in which we are incapable of doing so. As the German philosopher, Goethe put it, "It is entirely impossible for a thinking being to think of its own non-existence, of the termination of its own thinking and life." Indeed, for quite understandable reasons, there is tremendous denial of death in many Western cultures, as Ernest Becker famously argued. He writes, in his aptly titled classic, *The Denial of Death*, that

> "The individual has to protect himself against the world, and he can do this only as any other animal would: by narrowing down the world, shutting off experience, developing an obliviousness both to the terrors of the world and to his own anxieties. Otherwise he would be crippled for action."

Seen in this light, it shouldn't surprise us that—when it comes to facing the issue of his own mortality—our friend Daniel's response is to say, "I try not to go there!" But while he may run from death, Daniel can hardly hide. Many of his self-destructive behaviors may be understood as ways either of avoiding his "death anxiety," or of coping with it. For example, his affair with his young office assistant is a classic bit of acting out, for many men facing a "mid-life crisis." Indeed, in his book, *Staring at the Sun*, psychiatrist Dr. Irvin Yalom has argued that many such mid-life affairs are driven by a deep-seated fear of death. Better to run into the arms of an illicit lover than to be snatched by the arms of death! We may also understand Daniel's "panic attacks" and nightmares as attempts by his unconscious to deal with death anxiety. Yalom has gone so far as to claim that, "Most nightmares are fears of your personal death, and one wakens with . . . anxiety." ("Wise Counsel" interview with David Van Nuys, Ph.D). Yalom goes on to say that

> "It's not easy to live every moment wholly aware of
> death. It's like trying to stare the sun in the face: you
> can stand only so much of it. Because we cannot
> live frozen in fear, we generate methods to soften
> death's terror. We project ourselves into the future
> through our children; we grow rich, famous, ever
> larger; we develop compulsive protective rituals; or
> we embrace an impregnable belief in an ultimate
> rescuer." (*Staring at the Sun: Overcoming the Terror
> of Death*, p. 5)

In Daniel's case, the early loss of his mother may well have
intensified his fear of death. Furthermore, now that his children
have left home, a bit of his "future" has been taken away from
him—something we often describe as part of the "empty nest
syndrome".

We have now seen how all three of our traditions have dealt
with the stark inevitability of death—mainly by urging us to
acknowledge and confront our own mortality. The Stoics are
especially clear on this point, as when Marcus Aurelius urges,
"Since it is possible that you may depart from life this very moment,
regard every act and thought accordingly." We may endorse this
idea in principle, but perhaps with some reservations. Indeed,
there are quiet dissents from the classic Stoic position, even among
philosophers who are friends of the Stoic tradition. Michel de
Montaigne (1533-92), arguably the greatest confessional essayist
since St. Augustine, was profoundly influenced by the Stoics,
particularly Seneca. Yet Montaigne was suspicious of what he saw
as *undue emphasis* given to "preparing for death," in some Stoic
writings. Montaigne counsels us as follows:

> "Philosophy commands us to have death always
> before our eyes, to foresee it and to reflect upon it in

advance . . . [*but*] *if we have not known how to live, it is wrong to teach us how to die* . . . If we have known how to live steadfastly and calmly, we shall know how to die in the same way . . . Life should contain its own aim, its own purposes; its proper study is to regulate itself, guide itself and endure itself. Among the many duties included under . . . knowing how to live is this article of knowing how to die . . . [And yet] I have never found amongst my neighbors any peasant who deliberated on the bearing and assurance with which he would pass his final hours. Nature teaches him only to think of death when he is dying . . . we are always bothering ourselves by trying to forestall and control nature's ordinances. It is only the learned who let these thoughts spoil their dinners while they are in good health, and who scowl at the image of death. The common man has no need or remedy or consolation till the blow strikes; and he dwells on it only at the moment when he feels it." (Montaigne, 1958; italics added).

Perhaps Montaigne—having endured the untimely death of his dear friend, Étienne de la Boétie—is a bit *too* eager to banish any sort of "preparation" for death. Yet Montaigne's expressed wish regarding his own death contains at least as much wisdom as the pronouncements of the Stoics: "I want death to find me planting my cabbages, neither worrying about it, nor the unfinished gardening." (Essays I.20, cited in de Botton, p. 155). Another great philosopher heavily influenced by the Stoics, Baruch Spinoza (1632-77) put it this way: "The wise man thinks of death least of all things. His wisdom is a meditation on life."

*   *   *

Chapter 8

THE IMPORTANCE OF GRATITUDE

Judaism

"Ben Zoma says, Who is rich? One who rejoices in one's portion."

—Talmud, *Pirke Avot* 4.1

*"[The person] w*ho seeks more than he needs, hinders himself from enjoying what he has. Seek what you need and give up what you need not. For in giving up what you don't need, you'll learn what you really do need."

—Solomon ibn Gabirol, *Mivhar Hapeninim*

Ben Zoma . . . customarily said: "What labors did Adam have to carry out before he obtained bread to eat? He plowed. He sowed. He reaped. He bound the sheaves, threshed the grain . . . I, on the other hand, get up and find that all these things have already been done for me."

—Talmud, Berakhot 58a

Buddhism

"Let us rise up and be thankful, for if we didn't learn a lot today, at least we learned a little; and if we didn't learn a little, at least we didn't get sick; and if we got sick, at least we didn't die; so let us all be thankful."

—saying attributed to the Buddha

"A wise person who is grateful (*katannu*) and helps in return (*katavedi*); who is a noble friend and has a firm faith in what is good; who attentively serves those in distress; such a one is called a good person (*sappurisa*). Prosperity does not leave him who is endowed with all these good qualities."

—Jataka Sutta

"These two people are hard to find in the world . . . The one who is first to do a kindness, and the one who is grateful and thankful for a kindness done."

—The Buddha,
in the *Anguttara Nikaya* (AN 2:118).

Stoicism

"It is in no man's power to have whatever he wants; but he has it in his power not to wish for what he hasn't got, and cheerfully make the most of the things that do come his way.

—Seneca

"Any man who does not think that what he has is more than ample is an unhappy man, even if he is master of the whole world."

—Epicurus

"No deprivation is any trouble if you do not miss what you have lost."

—Cicero

"If you shape your life according to Nature, you will never be poor; if according to people's opinions, you will never be rich."

—Seneca

Izzy's Ingratitude

To his friends and acquaintances, Izzy was a man who "had it all." Raised in an Orthodox Jewish household, Izzy, age 52, had long ago abandoned Judaism and become, as he put it, "A full-fledged hedonist." Married, with two college-age children, and in good health, Izzy was a very successful hospital administrator. He had managed not only to run several area hospitals very efficiently, but also to accumulate a sizeable "nest egg." He and his family lived in a beautiful, 8-room, lakeside house, in a comfortable suburb of New York City. Izzy's wife, Rebecca, was a well-respected college professor, and both children were enrolled in prestigious, Ivy-league schools. Izzy managed to radiate a confident optimism that led nearly everyone to assume he was a very happy man—but the truth was entirely different.

As Izzy confided to his old college roommate, Hal, "I feel like I've gotten the short end of the stick, for all the work I've done. I mean, sure, I have a nice house, a good wife, great kids. But so what? Where is it getting me? I had the brains to go to medical school, but I wound up doing this damn administration crap! People at work are nice enough, but do they ever invite Rebecca and me to dinner, or out to a movie? No—it's all just business to them! And as for vacation, Hal, forget about it! The last one we took was two years ago, for exactly one week in Bermuda. I have people working under me who spend their whole summer in the Hamptons, or on the Cape! And Rebecca, she's a good wife, but she's not exactly what you'd call passionate, you know? I mean, I'm lucky to talk her into sex maybe once a week, at most." Although Izzy and Rebecca got along reasonably well, their marriage was marked by frequent arguments. Rebecca was not strictly observant in the Jewish faith, but she did like to keep active in her local synagogue, which offered a variety of social and educational activities. Izzy, however, refused to accompany her, arguing that, "Those people just want your time and money. All they care about is showing off."

Izzy and Rebecca had inherited several hundred thousand dollars from Izzy's parents, both of whom had died within the past five years, but Izzy had nothing good to say about his mother or father. "Sure!" he commented to Rebecca, "They left us a lot of money, but while they were alive, what did they do for us? All I ever got from my parents was criticism!"

As Rebecca confided to a close female friend, "Nothing is ever good enough with Izzy. We go out to a nice restaurant for a good time, and what does he do? He complains to the waiter! The roast beef is too stringy, the potatoes aren't hot enough, the service is too slow! We go to a movie, and he's ready to leave half-way through, because he thinks the movie is "stupid." He says he's proud of my accomplishments as a professor, but then he complains I'm spending too much time with my research. And does he ever have a good word to say about the kids? Here they are, both at Ivy League colleges, and Izzy says they're "wasting his hard earned money." Why? Because Joel is majoring in English Literature, and Laura is studying music theory. No matter how good things are, with Izzy, it's like there's always something wrong with it. Thank God, the doctor says Izzy is in good health, but he's always kvetching about how he can't play racquetball the way he used to when he was 30!"

The Perspective of Judaism

What we would call "gratitude" and "contentedness" correspond, respectively, to the Hebrew terms, *hakarat hatov* and *histapkut* (Telushkin 2000, Borowitz and Schwartz 1999). Together, these attributes might be subsumed under the English term, *thankfulness*. Rabbi Shlomo Toperoff points out that the epigram cited above, regarding "Who is rich?" (Pirke Avot 4:1) is not fundamentally about being "rich," but about being *happy* or contented. Rabbi Toperoff cites the words of the 13th century sage, Jacob Anatoli, who said, "If a man cannot get what he wants, he ought to want what he can get" (Toperoff 1997, 197). This Talmudic notion of happiness, as Toperoff points out, stresses the "great attribute of thankfulness." Without thankfulness and gratitude, it is impossible to conceive of "the flourishing life." Indeed, we find Izzy almost devoid of happiness or fulfillment. He is cut off even from those he professes to care for, such as his wife. In contrast, the person of gratitude does not dissipate energy fuming and griping about what is lacking. As one Mussar lesson puts it, "Not focusing on trying to fulfill never-ending needs and desires frees us to be fully present [in] the moment and available to the others in our lives." (http://www.mussarleadership.org/pdfs/Histapkut-Temperance.pdf.)

Lori Palatnik (2000) has observed that, "Being a Jew is synonymous with expressing gratitude." Indeed, Jews are instructed to begin each day with a prayer of thankfulness, known as the *modeh ani*. In English, the prayer goes, "Thankful am I before you, living and eternal King, that you have returned my soul within me with compassion, abundant is Your faithfulness." You might wonder what the term "faithfulness" (*emunah*) has to do with *thankfulness*. The Rabbis tell us that, in effect, *we return God's faithfulness with our own* by expressing a prayer of thanksgiving each day. (http://www.aish.com/48945526.html)

Yet all too often, we fail to appreciate all that has been given us, or how our fellow human beings have contributed to what we have. In the words of Ben Zoma, part of whose teaching we cited at the beginning of this chapter,

> "What labors did Adam have to carry out before he obtained bread to eat? He plowed. He sowed. He reaped. He bound the sheaves, threshed the grain, winnowed the chaff, selected the ears, ground them, sifted the flour, kneaded the dough, and baked it. Only then was he able to eat. I, on the other hand, get up and find that all these things have already been done for me. Similarly, how many labors did Adam have to carry out before he obtained a garment to wear? He had to shear the sheep, wash the wool, comb it, spin it, and weave it. Then did he have a garment to wear. All I have to do is get up and find that these things too have been done for me."
> (Berakhot 58a; in Dorff, 2005, 102-3)

Judaism teaches us to appreciate even the most basic functions of the body, such as our normal bowel and bladder functions. As one Talmudic blessing puts it:

"Praised are You, Lord our God, King of the
universe, who with wisdom fashioned the human
body, creating openings, arteries, glands and
organs . . . should but one of them, by being blocked
or opened, fail to function, it would be impossible
to exist. Praised are You, Lord, healer of all flesh who
sustains our bodies in wondrous ways." (Sherwin
and Cohen, p. 17).

Thus, when we find ourselves amidst the sick and injured,
whose bodies do not function, we might remind ourselves of
the Yiddish proverb, "If you can't be grateful for what you have
received, then be thankful for what you have been spared."

Indeed, Dr. Alan Moranis, a lecturer on the Mussar tradition
of Judaism, tells us that,

"The Mussar teachings on . . . gratitude are tough,
because they don't let us feel sorry for ourselves, no
matter how little we may have. One Mussar master
began a talk with a thump on the table and the words,
"It is enough that a human being is alive!" Then he
ended his talk right there." (Moranis, "Gratitude,"
http://www.jewishpathways.com/mussar-program/
gratitude)

Compare that attitude with Izzy's griping over his diminished
skill, playing racquetball! In Yiddish, Izzy represents what is
commonly known as a "kvetch", of whom Leo Rosten wrote:
"The *kvetch* can never be satisfied; for the *kvetch*, nothing ever
goes right."

In Western society, we often associated well-being with
material possessions, such as a fine house or a nice car. But for the
sages of Hasidism, gratitude is much more a state of mind than

a function of material wealth. A more homely way of expressing this idea is nicely summarized in a Jewish folk tale, as told by Eugene Borowitz and Francine Schwartz:

> "Once a poor Hasid became so distraught because of the overcrowding in his hovel that he appealed to his Rebbe, "We have so many people living with us that we can't turn around in the house." The Rebbe counseled the man . . . [to move his goat, then his chickens, and then his cow] into the house. [The man] returned, half crazed, to the Rebbe. "It's the end of the world," cried the man. The Rebbe responded, "Now go home, turn out the goat, chickens and cow, and report to me tomorrow." The following day the Hasid showed up beaming. "Rebbe! My hut seems like a palace now!'" (Borowitz & Schwartz, pp. 164-5)

The wisdom of this teaching may be summed up in a Yiddish proverb: "If a Jew breaks a leg, he thanks God he did not break both legs. If he breaks both legs, he thanks God he did not break his neck." (modified from Gribetz 2004, 137).

The Buddhist Perspective

In the discourse known as the *Mangala Sutta*, the Buddha declares *gratitude* (in Pali, *katannuta*) to be one of the highest blessings—one that plays a key role in Buddhist ethics. Thus, in Verse 8, we read, "Reverence, humility, contentment, bearing gratitude and opportune hearing of the Dhamma; this is Blessing Supreme." [Nalanda Institute; http://nalanda.org.my/e-library/mangalasutta/verse8.php]

Phillip Moffit—a former publishing executive who became an ordained *vipassana* (insight) meditation teacher—has many wise things to say about gratitude, and he merits a lengthy quotation:

> "The Buddha taught that every human birth is precious and worthy of gratitude. In one of his well-known analogies, he said that receiving a human birth is [rarer] than the chance that a blind turtle floating in the ocean would stick its head through a small hoop. He would often instruct a monk to take his ground cloth into the forest, sit at the base of a tree, and begin "gladdening the heart" by reflecting on the series of fortunate circumstances that had given the monk the motivation and ability to seek freedom through understanding the dharma.

> Practicing mindfulness of gratitude consistently leads to a direct experience of being connected to life and the realization that there is a larger context in which your personal story is unfolding. Being relieved of the endless wants and worries of your life's drama, even temporarily, is liberating. Cultivating thankfulness for being part of life blossoms into a feeling of being blessed, not in the sense of winning the lottery, but in a more refined appreciation for the interdependent nature of life. It also elicits feelings of generosity, which create further joy . . . Having access to the joy and wonderment of life is the antidote to feelings of scarcity and loss. It allows you to meet life's difficulties with an open heart. The understanding you gain from practicing gratitude frees you from being lost or identified with either

the negative or the positive aspects of life, letting you simply meet life in each moment as it rises. (Phillip Moffitt http://www.lifebalanceinstitute. com/dharmawisdom/articles/selfless-gratitude-0)

Thanissaro Bhikkhu, the abbot of San Diego County's Metta Forest Monastery, makes an important distinction in discussing gratitude. There is, on the one hand, "appreciation of a general sort"—for example, the way we might appreciate our warm, cozy house in the winter. On the other hand, there is "gratitude in particular", which the Buddha always linked with our *response to kindness*. As Thanissaro Bhikkhu puts it,

> "You feel indebted to the people who helped you because you sense how easily they might have denied that help, and how difficult your life might have been if that's what they had chosen to do. Your parents, for instance, didn't *have* to raise you, or arrange for someone else to raise you; they could have aborted you or left you to die. So the fact that you're alive to read this means that somebody chose, again and again, to help you when you were helpless. Sensing that element of choice is what creates your sense of debt." http://shambhalasun. com/sunspace/?p=19864

In Pali, the word for "grateful"—*kataññu*—literally means "to have a sense of what was done"—as in, acts of kindness that were done in our behalf (Davids & Steeds, 1993). **Thanissaro Bhikkhu** teaches that those who have shown us kindness are owed not merely appreciation, but *a debt of gratitude*. For example, ". . . the way to repay a teacher's compassion and sympathy in teaching you is to apply yourself to learning your lessons well." Similarly, it is not enough merely to "appreciate" that your parents taught you to be a kind person—you must repay the debt of gratitude to your parents by being kind to others. (http://shambhalasun.com/sunspace/?p=19856).

Now, in contrast to *katannuta* (gratitude), we have *akatannuta* or *ingratitude*. The Buddhist monk, the Venerable Nyanadassana, defines *akatannuta* as ". . . not knowing or recognizing what has been done . . . for one's benefit." So why do some develop this negative attitude? Nyanadassana opines that,

> "There are many reasons but the four most important ones why ingratitude arises are: 1. failure to recognize a benefit as a benefit; 2.taking benefits for granted; 3. egotism; [and] 4. forgetfulness. There are some people who do not regard life itself as a benefit. Hence, they don't feel grateful to their parents for bringing them into the world . . . similarly, there are people who don't regard knowledge or education or culture as benefits. So they do not feel grateful towards their teachers . . . They may even feel resentful . . . This attitude is, of course, very widespread in society today. People tend to think that everything is due to them." http://www.buddhistelibrary.org/library/view.php?adpath=360)

We see these forms of ingratitude in nearly everything Izzy complains about, including his total lack of appreciation for his parents (and the largesse they left him); his resentment toward those he sees as "better off" than he; and his strong sense of entitlement. In many ways, Izzy fits the description of the proverbial person ". . . who was born on third base and believes he must have hit a triple!" And because Izzy seems incapable of appreciating all that he has, and all that has been given to him, he has also denied himself "access to the joy and wonderment of life."

The Stoic Perspective

One of our opening epigrams is from Epicurus: "Any man who does not think that what he has is more than ample is an unhappy man, even if he is master of the whole world." This teaching has obvious application to our unfortunate friend, Izzy, whose nearly total lack of gratitude has indeed left him a very "unhappy man" indeed.

Epicurus was actually not a Stoic in the strict sense; rather, he was the founder of a competing school of philosophy, contemporaneous with the Stoics. Epicureanism and Stoicism had many beliefs in common, but held different attitudes toward our participation in the larger community. Whitney J. Oates, in contrasting Stoicism with Epicureanism, tells us that, "The two systems are alike in that they attempt to give men peace and inner calm." But whereas Epicureanism recommended ". . . a retirement into the garden, in order to gain that peace," the Stoics maintained ". . . that the peace must be found in the midst of the world's confusions for, after all, all men are brothers." (The Stoic and Epicurean Philosophers, Modern Library edition, p. xxiv.) In this sense, the Stoics have something in common with Judaism's *Hasidim*, who believe that one can worship God in everyday life, even amidst the hurly-burly of the market place.

Notwithstanding these differences, the quote from Epicurus—"Any man who does not think that what he has is more than ample is an unhappy man . . ."—is quintessentially Stoic in spirit. Indeed, gratitude is one of the most important values in Stoic philosophy, though it is often given short shrift in discussions of Stoicism.

We see the importance of gratitude when Marcus Aurelius begins his *Meditations* with a litany of "thank you" notes. Marcus thanks everybody from his paternal grandfather to the gods! For example:

> *"Courtesy and serenity of temper I first learnt to know from my grandfather Verus . . . Manliness without ostentation I learnt from what I have heard and remember of my father . . . My mother set me an example of piety and generosity . . ."*

As Farquharson puts it, these notes of thanks comprise ". . . a personal acknowledgment of lessons learned and good gifts received from the men and women who seemed . . . to have had the most influence on his life . . ." (op cit. p. 95).

In this respect, Marcus Aurelius is a kind of "anti-Izzy!"

Similarly, Seneca tells us, "It is in no man's power to have whatever he wants; but he has it in his power not to wish for what he hasn't got, and cheerfully make the most of the things that do come his way." He writes these words in a letter (CXXIII) to his younger friend, Lucilius, having returned home after a long and tiring journey. Seneca notes that, ". . . I'm in bed, recovering from my fatigue, and making the best of [the] slowness on the part of the cook . . ." adding, ". . . whatever kind of meal is on the way is going to beat an inaugural banquet for enjoyment." Seneca here demonstrates that our sense of fulfillment and satisfaction is largely a matter of our perspective; and that we can indeed be grateful even when life is not providing us with banquets. (Of course, few of us are fortunate enough to have our own cook!). In another letter, Seneca quotes a fragment attributed to the moralist, Publilius Syrus (1st century BCE): "The poor lack much, the greedy everything." This maxim may serve as a synopsis of the Stoic view of gratitude, as well as a sad commentary on people like Izzy.

We have already discussed some of Cicero's writings on "old age", and our epigram ("No deprivation is any trouble if you do not miss what you have lost") is drawn from Cicero's essay titled, "The Pleasures of Old Age." There, Cicero sets out to discredit the notion that the elderly are less capable of enjoyment than the young. (Here we think of Izzy's petulant complaint that he can no longer play racquetball the way he did when he was 20 years younger!). Cicero concedes that when it comes to sexual pleasure, old age is at a disadvantage; e.g., ". . . let us admit that youth exceeds age in its enjoyment of this particular kind of pleasure." But then Cicero quickly shifts perspective to see a deeper kind of pleasure in old age. He writes,

> "When its campaigns of sex, ambition, rivalry, quarrelling, and all the other passions are ended, the human spirit returns to live within itself—and is well off. There is supreme satisfaction to be derived from an old age which has knowledge and learning to feed upon . . . surely the satisfactions of the mind are greater than all the rest!" ("On Old Age" in *Selected Works*)

Indeed, for the Stoics, we might summarize the "flourishing life" in this way: We live best when we strive to gather knowledge; live in harmony with Nature; act in an ethical manner; and experience gratitude for whatever blessings life has given us.

Synthesis and Commentary

Mark Twain once quipped that, "A self-made man is about as likely as a self-laid egg." Indeed, as Rabbi Byron L. Sherwin and Rabbi Seymour J. Cohen have noted, "Gratitude to God is an acknowledgment that *no one is self-made*." (p. 15, italics added).

The French philosopher Andre Comte-Sponville, in his excellent book, *A Small Treatise on the Great Virtues*, has this to say about gratitude:

> "What gratitude teaches us . . . is that there is also such a thing as joyful humility, or humble joy, humble because it knows it is not its own cause . . . and, knowing this, rejoices all the more . . ." (op cit, p. 135).

Gratitude, indeed, may be the deepest wisdom. As Epicurus puts it, "The fool's life is empty of gratitude and full of fears . . ." While we won't condemn Izzy as a "fool"—after all, as Albert Ellis would remind us, labeling someone in that way does injustice to the person's humanity and potential for change—many of Izzy's ideas and attitudes are certainly foolish. For example, Izzy's grumbling that he hasn't had a vacation in two years would strike many hard-working, or unemployed, Americans as laughable self-pity! The Buddhist sages would call Izzy's gripe a form of *upadana*—a "grasping onto things" (Ajahn Chah, *Living Dhamma*, p. 36). The Stoics would regard it as weak-kneed, self-indulgence. The Rabbis of the Talmud would simply be mystified (as in, "What is this *vacation* thing?"), while our modern rabbis would call it "kvetching", plain and simple!

Perhaps, as Epicurus' saying suggests, there is an underlying fear in Izzy's litany of complaints. In our previous chapter, we discussed the fear of death, and how it may be repressed, denied, or acted out through various defensive maneuvers—as we saw with Daniel's mid-life affair (Chapter 7). Constant complaining about what one lacks may also serve a defensive function—it fends off anxiety about one's own mortality, and focuses one's ire and energy on "those other people", who have "everything." In Izzy's case, complaining also fends off the question, "*Why is it that I can't seem to find real happiness?"* by laying the blame on "those other people" such as Izzy's parents. Ironically, the cause of Izzy's inability to find happiness is . . . Izzy! The medieval philosopher, Solomon ibn Gabirol, sums up Izzy's predicament very succinctly: "[He] who seeks more than he needs, hinders himself from enjoying what he has." And there are few more effective ways of avoiding constructive action than complaining about our many woes.

Finally, the Talmud instructs us that, "Even a poor man who himself survives on charity should give charity." *(Babylonian Talmud, Gittin 7b).* This is not only an ethical imperative; it is also a deep psychological insight. Paradoxically, one way we feel that we "have enough" is to *give things away*—ideally, to others who may be less fortunate. Often, we are richest when we give away some deep-seated part of ourselves—such as our time, love or effort. In this way, we gather spiritual wealth. The philosopher John Stuart Mill put it this way:

> "Those . . . who are happy . . . have their minds
> fixed on some object other than their own happiness;
> on the happiness of others, on the improvement of
> mankind, even on some art or pursuit . . . aiming thus
> at something else, they find happiness by the way."

Chapter 9

SELF-MASTERY AND ANGER

Judaism

Getting angry is like worshipping idols.

> —*Midrash LeOlam*

Ben Zoma says: Who is mighty? One who conquers one's passions, as it is said: "One who is slow to anger is better than the mighty, and one who rules over one's spirit is better than one who conquers a city"

> —(Proverbs 16:32, Pirke Avot 4:1)

"When I feel angry against a person, I delay the expression of my anger. I say to myself: 'What will I lose if I postpone my anger?'"

> —the Rozdoler Rabbi

"Hence [you learn] that the Holy One, blessed be He, says prayers. What does He pray? . . . [God prays] 'May it be My will that My mercy may suppress My anger . . .'" (Talmud, Berakoth 7a).

Buddhism

"He who can control his rising anger as a coachman controls his carriage at full speed, this man I call a good driver . . . :

—Dhammapada 222 (Mascaro, p. 68).

"A man is not on the path of righteousness if he settles matters in a violent haste. A wise man calmly considers what is right and what is wrong, and faces different opinions with truth, non-violence, and peace."

—Dhammapada 19:256-7 (Mascaro p. 73).

"Forsake anger, give up pride. Sorrow cannot touch the man who is not in the bondage of anything . . ."

—Dhammapada 17:221 (Mascaro, p. 68).

". . . patience is the antidote to anger and aggression . . . patience means getting smart: you stop and wait."

—Pema Chödrön

"Holding on to anger is like drinking poison and expecting the other person to die."

—the Buddha

Stoicism

"Anger carried to excess begets madness."

—Epicurus (quoted by Seneca)

"What's the use of overcoming opponent after opponent . . . if you can be overcome by your temper?"

—Seneca

"How much more grievous are the consequences of anger than the causes of it."

—Marcus Aurelius, *Meditations*

"Whenever you lose your temper or become upset about something . . . you're forgetting that everything is what your opinion makes it, and that the present moment is all you have, to live and lose."

—Marcus Aurelius, *Meditations*

Vignette: Felicity's Fury

Felicity was a 30-year-old, unmarried lab technician, who entered psychotherapy with the complaint, "People just can't handle my honesty!" She had been referred by her employer, after a supervisor had given Felicity a poor performance evaluation. Although her technical skills were described as "excellent," her social and interpersonal skills were rated as "poor." The supervisor had commented, "Ms. X, one of our senior lab techs, has difficulties relating respectfully to her co-workers, as well as to her supervisors. She tends to become hostile and verbally abusive when her judgment is challenged, or her work criticized. She is extremely impatient with others and will lash into them if they do not comply with her wishes immediately. She seems unable to appreciate the feelings or sensitivities of others, and tends to see them as useful "drones," here to serve her needs. In one instance, Ms. X actually threw a laboratory beaker at one of her assistants, because the latter was late with a routine blood test result." Upon reading a copy of this report, Felicity first contemplated a law suit for "defamation of character" and "harassment", against her employer. However, upon discussing the issue with her older sister—"The only person I've ever really gotten along with"—Felicity reluctantly agreed to enter psychotherapy.

Felicity was the younger of two daughters born to a professor of philosophy, and a math teacher—parents Felicity described as ". . . as warm and nurturing as barbed wire on a cactus." She related how, as a young girl, her mother would tell her to "buck up" whenever Felicity complained of being unhappy or angry. "If I threw a tantrum, my parents would just ignore me until I either shut up or gave up," she told her therapist. She added, "I've never really forgiven them for that."

Felicity described her difficulty in meeting men and making close friends. "I guess people see me as too judgmental, but the way I see it, they just don't want to hear any criticism." She acknowledged that she had "trouble getting close to anyone", and added, "I wish people would be a little more appreciative of what I have to offer. I don't think they realize that I can see solutions to problems that nobody else even dreams of—like the time, in the lab, I figured out why we were getting false positive readings on a blood test, and my idiot supervisor didn't have a clue! If people can't respect me for what I am, they can go to hell!" But despite her apparent bravado, Felicity acknowledged that at times, "I wonder if I'm kind of a louse—that maybe I'm just not deserving of being liked, much less loved." At this point in her session, Felicity seemed to be on the verge of tears.

The Jewish Perspective

Judaism in general and the Talmud in particular place a high value on self-restraint—especially on the *control of anger*. The one who is overwhelmed with rage is likened to an idol-worshipper; thus, the Talmud teaches that ". . . one who tears his clothes and destroys his property in his fury is as one who worships idols (Shabbos 105b). In what sense is the enraged person like an idol-worshipper? The Talmud tell us that, "He who loses his temper, even the Divine Presence is unimportant in his eyes, as it is written, The wicked, through the pride of his countenance, will not seek God . . ." (Nedarim 22b). As Sherwin and Cohen observe,

> "Anger places the ego at the center, displacing God and others, and causing the alienation of relationships." (p. 84, *Creating an Ethical Jewish Life*).

It seems clear that for the Rabbis, the "idol" being worshipped by the angry person is himself or herself! This connection between anger and narcissism is evident in Felicity's grandiose and demanding attitude. We'll have more to say about *pathological narcissism* and anger in the "Synthesis and Commentary" section.

The Rabbis are especially keen to eliminate the terribly destructive effects of unbridled rage, which is seen almost as a kind of mind-destroying, altered state of consciousness. In *Proverbs* (14:29), we are taught that, "He who is slow to anger has great understanding, but he who has a hasty temper exalts folly." And the Talmud teaches that, "He who loses his temper is exposed to all of the torments of hell" (Nedarim 22a). Similarly, as the ancient guide to ethics, *Orhot Zaddikim*, puts it:

"You often see people who, when they are angry . . .
are not conscious of what they are doing and do
many things in their anger which they would not
do if they were free from anger; for anger draws out
the intelligence of a person . . . until his angry deeds
multiply and he is plunged into strife and quarrel."
(cited in Sherwin & Cohen, p. 84).

And yet, despite all these condemnations of anger, there is
some ambivalence in the rabbinical literature. On the one hand,
the Vilna Gaon believed that anger ". . . must be totally eradicated,
as it has almost no redeeming value." (Lieber 1995, 213). On the
other hand, the word "almost" is important here. Maimonides,
in the *Mishneh Torah* (Twersky, 1972, p. 54) describes anger
as "an exceedingly bad passion, and one should avoid it to the
last extreme." But even Maimonides concedes the occasional
value of *simulating* anger, as when one wants to discipline one's
children—so long as one "does not really feel" anger. Thus,
Maimonides seems to say that anger is not an *inherently evil*
emotion; but rather, a passion *to be bridled and mastered* so that
one doesn't truly "feel" it—a bit like taming and bridling a wild
stallion!

Similarly, Rabbi Shlomo Toperoff notes that *erekh
apayim*—being *slow to anger*—is "one of the thirteen attributes
of God" (Toperoff 1997, 280). Notably, the Talmud does not
admonish us, "Never get angry!" Rather, Ben Zoma urges us to
be "*slow* to anger," and Rabbi Eliezer instructs us, "do not anger
easily" (Pirke Avot 2:15). Indeed, Lieber wisely observes, it is
really impossible never to get angry, so the mishnah (Pirke Avot
2:15) instructs us not to anger *easily*. We must be level-headed
enough to assess whether the incident that sparked our anger
is sufficient cause for expressing how we feel. Furthermore, we
should actively attempt to find reasons *not* to be angry (Lieber

1995, 106). As the Rozdoler Rebbe is said to have commented: "When I feel angry against a person, I delay the expression of my anger. I say to myself: `What will I lose if I postpone my anger?" (*Niflaot ha-Rebbe*).

More radically, *Orhot Zaddikim* also discusses a "positive" side to anger. As Sherwin and Cohen put it, ". . . anger is a necessary spur to survival, and anger is a necessary stimulus in confronting evil and evil people." (p. 252). Perhaps anger of a certain highly-refined type may fit this formulation—but certainly not beaker-throwing "hissy fits" such as we saw with Felicity! Even in those rare circumstances when it may be a *mitzvah* (commandment) to show anger—for example, when there is a public breach of the law—our expression of anger "should be done like all other *mitzvos*—calmly and with much forethought" (Lieber 1995, 106). In short: the rabbis hand us the complicated task of showing, at most, a highly restrained and nearly "rational" form of anger.

This is clearly not an easy line to walk. Indeed, the rabbis are under no illusions regarding our ability to control our anger. Even God needs "help" sometimes! The Talmud reveals this in a fascinating passage: "Hence [you learn] that the Holy One, blessed be He, says prayers. What does He pray?—R. Zutra b. Tobi said in the name of Rab: 'May it be My will that My mercy may suppress My anger, and that My mercy may prevail over My [other] attributes, so that I may deal with My children in the attribute of mercy . . ." (Talmud, Berakoth 7a).

I believe the message is not only one concerning God, but also one directed at humanity; namely, "*If God Himself gets angry, don't be too hard on yourself for doing so*, nor should you imagine that you will ever eliminate your anger completely." This is part of the "anti-perfectionism" inherent in Judaism. At the same time, it is clear that when God *does* get angry, it is only for a fraction of a second:

"Our Rabbis taught: God is angry every day,
but how long does His anger last?—A moment.
And how long is a moment?—one fifty three
thousand eight hundred forty eighth of an hour is
a moment.—Abodah Zarah Folio 4a [http://www.
come-and-hear.com/]

This interval is around .06 seconds, by my calculation! So—if *imitatio dei*—emulating God—is a cardinal tenet of Judaism, the lesson is clear: we can't eliminate anger entirely, but our anger should be *exceedingly brief.* That said, throwing a beaker at somebody—however brief the act—would definitely not be countenanced by the rabbis!

The Buddhist Perspective

Along with *greed* and *ignorance*, Buddhism considers *anger* one of the "three poisons." Together, these toxic qualities are believed to be the primary causes of *samsara*—the eternal cycle of birth, death, and rebirth. Cleansing ourselves of anger is essential to Buddhist practice, and Buddhist philosophy denies any such thing as "righteous" or "justifiable" anger. (Barbara O'Brien, http://buddhism.about.com/od/basicbuddhistteachings/a/anger. htm). Thus, none of Felicity's self-serving rationalizations for losing her temper would hold water in Buddhist circles!

And where does anger originate? Not in things or events outside ourselves, but in our own *manner of relating* to such externals. As Ajahn Chah puts it,

"All things are just as they are . . . the thorn is just
minding its own business, it doesn't harm anybody.
Only if you step on the thorn will you suffer over

it . . . all the things in this world are simply there as
they are. It's we who pick fights with them. And if we
hit them they're going to hit us back. If they're left
on their own they won't bother anybody; only the
swaggering drunkard gives them trouble." (*Living
Dhamma* p. 110)

Buddhist sages also trace anger to the underlying attitude of
self-centeredness—reminiscent of the rabbinical view that anger is
akin to self-worship, and certainly relevant to Felicity's character
flaws. The Tibetan meditation master, the Venerable Lobsang
Gyatso, makes this point clear:

> "The self-centered attitude is the empowering
> condition which promotes pride and incorrect
> views . . . it also endeavors to conceal our faults while
> drawing attention to our good qualities. It shows no
> tolerance of even the slightest mistakes that others
> may have made with respect to us. Instead, causing
> anger, [the self-centered attitude] induces all of our
> personal shortcomings and sustains the attitude
> that we are superior to others . . . due to it, we are
> jealous of our betters, competitive with our equals,
> and belittling toward our inferiors. It is . . . like a
> malignant disease . . . ensuring that we fail to achieve
> any worthwhile long-term goals." (from *Bodhicitta*,
> pp. 61-62).

This passage is virtually a synopsis of Felicity's way of relating
to others, whom she views as either "drones" or idiots! It also
points out the self-defeating nature of persistently angry behavior.
So what, then, is the Buddhist response to anger? How are we to
deal with anger in our own lives? First, let's consider the Buddhist

view of what *not* to do when you are feeling angry. As Thich Nhat Hanh puts it in a vivid analogy,

> "If your house is on fire, the most urgent thing to do is to go back and try to put out the fire, not to run after the person you believe to be the arsonist. If you run after the person you suspect has burned your house, your house will burn down while you are chasing him or her . . . You must go back and put out the fire. So when you are angry, if you continue to interact with or argue with the other person, if you try to punish her, you are acting exactly like someone who runs after the arsonist while everything goes up in flames." (from *Anger: Wisdom for Cooling the Flames,* p. 24)

OK—so engaging in verbal (much less actual) fisticuffs is not the answer. Then what *should* we do when we feel that someone has "made" us angry? The prominent Buddhist teacher, Pema Chodron, believes that *patience* and *self-awareness* are the foundation stones for controlling our anger. At the same time, it's important not to "beat up" on ourselves for feeling anger:

> "The Buddhist teachings tell us that patience is the antidote to anger and aggression. When we feel aggression in all its many forms—resentment, bitterness, being very critical, complaining and so forth . . . Patience has a lot to do with getting smart at that point and just waiting: not speaking or doing anything." (http://www.shambhalasun.com/index.php?option=content&task=view&id=1309)

Here we recall the Rozdoler Rabbi's comment: "What will I lose if I postpone my anger?" Pema Chodron continues:

> "On the other hand, [patience] also means being completely and totally honest with yourself about the fact that you're furious. You're not suppressing anything—patience has nothing to do with suppression. In fact, it has everything to do with a gentle, honest relationship with yourself . . . you can be honest about the fact that you're angry. But at the same time you can . . . let go of the internal dialogue. In that dialogue you are blaming and criticizing, and then probably feeling guilty and beating yourself up for doing that . . . It's painful to experience such awful confusion. Still, you just wait and remain patient with your confusion and the pain that comes with it." (http://www.shambhalasun.com/index.php ?option=content&task=view&id=1309)

Finally, Thich Nhat Hanh reminds us that we may be quite mistaken as to the "cause" of our anger. Before blaming the other person, we ought to be sure we know what is really going on! For example, you may believe that someone has been "gossiping" about you, only to learn that he was inquiring after your health, and that you were upsetting yourself for no reason:

> "While embracing your anger, you [should] practice looking deeply to see the nature of your anger, because you . . . may be the victim of a wrong perception. You may have misunderstood what you heard and saw. You may have a wrong idea of what had been said, what had been done. . . . You remember that you should not be so sure that you

are the victim of the other person's wrongdoing . . .
You yourself may have created the hell inside you."
(*Anger: Wisdom for Cooling the Flames, p. 59*)

The Stoic Perspective

Like the Rabbis of the Talmud, the Stoics were keenly aware
of the destructive effects of anger. Given the violent and brutal
times the Roman Stoics lived in—Cicero (106 BCE-43 BCE) was
murdered by his political enemies, and Seneca (ca. 4 BCE-65 CE)
was forced to commit suicide by the Emperor Nero!—perhaps we
can understand the Stoics' antipathy toward anger. They would
certainly be dismayed, if not disgusted, by Felicity's "hostile and
verbally abusive" behavior.

Cicero emphasized the *antisocial* aspects of anger, and sought
to counteract that effect through courtesy and tact. Thus, he tells
us that

> ". . . as we have a most excellent rule for every phase
> of life, to avoid exhibitions of passion . . . let there
> be no exhibition of anger or inordinate desire . . .
> We must also take the greatest care to show courtesy
> and consideration toward those with whom we
> converse. It may sometimes happen that there is
> need of administering reproof. On such occasions,
> we should, perhaps, use a more emphatic tone of
> voice . . . and even assume an appearance of being
> angry. But we shall [never] have recourse to this sort
> of reproof . . . unless it is unavoidable and no other
> remedy can be discovered. We may seem angry, but
> anger should be far from us; for in anger, nothing
> right or judicious can be done."—"On Duties"

(This use of "feigned anger" is reminiscent of Maimonides, cited above, though I'm not aware of any evidence that Maimonides had read Cicero).

Seneca seems more vehement than Cicero in his condemnation of anger. In his classic work, *On Anger* [*De Ira*], Seneca minces no words in describing his revulsion at this emotion. He calls anger ". . . the most hideous and frenzied of all the emotions. For the other emotions have in them some element of peace and calm, while this one is wholly violent . . ." http://facultypages.morris. umn.edu/~mcollier/Intro%20to%20Philosophy/Seneca.pdf

Seneca observes that, "Certain wise men . . . have claimed that anger is temporary madness . . . [and] you have only to behold the expressions of those possessed by anger to know that they are insane." Similarly, in his letters to Lucilius, Seneca quotes Epicurus to the effect that "Anger carried to excess begets madness." Seneca adds: "It is true . . . the outcome of violent anger is a mental raving, and therefore anger is to be avoided, not for the sake of moderation, but for the sake of sanity." (Letter XVIII) Furthermore, Seneca's indictment continues, ". . . if you choose to view [anger's] results and the harm of it, no plague has cost the human race more dearly."

Seneca does not place much value on the ability to triumph over one's external enemies, if one is defeated by that terrible *internal* foe, anger. He writes, in another letter, "What's the use of overcoming opponent after opponent . . . if you can be overcome by your temper?" In this attitude, Seneca is close in spirit to the Talmudic teaching** that asks, "Who is mighty? The one who restrains his passions . . . [for] one who rules over one's spirit is better than one who conquers a city." (Pirke Avot 4:1). Thus, Seneca writes, in letter LXXXVIII, "Humanity is the quality which stops one being arrogant toward one's fellows, or being acrimonious."

Perhaps Seneca's chief contribution to the Stoic perspective on anger is his distinction between anger over *injustices peculiar to oneself*, and *those that affect all human beings*; e.g.,

> "Resent a thing by all means if it represents an injustice decreed against yourself personally; but if this same constant is binding on the lowest and highest alike, then make your peace again with destiny." *(Letters from a Stoic,* pp. 181-82).

Indeed, Seneca asks us to imagine Nature addressing us as follows: "Those things you grumble about are the same for everyone. I can give no one anything easier."

Marcus Aurelius (121-180 CE)—like Cicero and Seneca—lived in a violent and turbulent age and spent much of his political career on the battlefield. There, he must have gained a keen appreciation of the dangers of anger. In his Meditations, Marcus writes, "There is but one thing of real value—to cultivate truth and justice, and to live without anger in the midst of lying and unjust men." Indeed, Marcus insists that, "I cannot be angry with a brother or resent him, for we were born into this world to work together like the feet, hands, eyelids and lower rows of teeth . . ." (*Meditations,* Hicks p. 27). Like modern cognitive-behavioral therapists, Marcus was aware that we are often provoked to anger by trivial and passing irritations, which, however, may have serious adverse effects. He writes, "Our rage and lamentations do us more harm than whatever caused our anger and grief in the first place." (from *The Emperor's Handbook: A New Translation of the Meditations,* by David Hicks, C. Scott Hicks).

Marcus also sees anger in the larger, spiritual context of the human community, and its function in the larger order of the universe. He writes that,

"Whenever you lose your temper or become upset about something, you're forgetting that everything serves the purpose of the whole; that another's wrong is not your concern; and that whatever causes you to be upset has always happened and will always happen and even now is happening everywhere. You are also forgetting that what binds humankind to one another is not blood and family ties, but the community of mind. You're forgetting too that everyone's mind is of God and flows from the same divine source . . . Finally, you're forgetting that everything is what your opinion makes it, and that the present moment is all you have, to live and lose" (p. 140 from Hicks and Hicks; Book 11, *Meditations*)

Synthesis and Commentary

The Jewish tradition sees anger as closely linked with what modern psychologists would call *narcissism*. As we noted earlier, Sherwin and Cohen observe that, "Anger places the ego at the center, displacing God and others, and causing the alienation of relationships." (p. 84, *Creating an Ethical Jewish Life*). This certainly seems true in the case of Felicity, whose anger is closely linked with her profound sense of superiority and entitlement. But, as with many narcissistically-disordered persons, Felicity's veneer of angry hauteur conceals an inner core of insecurity and low self-esteem. Indeed, she acknowledges that, at times, she wonders if she a "louse", and undeserving of others' love and respect. Dr. Giancarlo Dimaggio has described (*Psychiatric Times* 7/18/12) the connection between narcissism and anger;

specifically, individuals with full-blown Narcissistic Personality Disorder (NPD) often show intense outbursts of anger

> ". . . triggered by feelings of social rejection and . . . [by] those who give negative feedback. Persons with NPD often feel hampered in pursuing goals and blame others for being inept, incompetent, or hostile. States in which the self-image is extremely negative . . . are so hard to bear that fighting with others and blaming them for any personal flaws is a more suitable defensive maneuver. When shortcomings are impossible to deny (eg, being fired from work, breaking affective bonds), persons with NPD are likely to become depressed."

Prof. Dimaggio also notes that while "There is no consensus on the causes of NPD . . . lack of parental empathy toward a child's developmental needs may bear some responsibility. In the context of disturbed attachment, parents may fail to appropriately recognize, name, and regulate the child's emotions, particularly in cases of heightened arousal." Research also suggests that, among narcissistic adolescents, the experience of being "shamed"—often a consequence of bullying by peers—may trigger bouts of "humiliated fury" (Thomaes et al, Emotion, 2011 11:786-93).

All this is just to say that we can partially "explain" certain cases of intense and persistent anger in psychological terms, by invoking the concept of pathological narcissism. But *explanations are not excuses*, and none of the great teachers in our three traditions would give Felicity a "free pass" simply because she was raised in a home with unaffectionate or withholding parents! Like present-day cognitive psychologists—notably, the late Dr. Albert Ellis—the sages of Judaism, Buddhism and Stoicism would all argue that with sufficient discipline, effort and practice, even disadvantaged individuals can overcome the negative experiences of childhood, and gain control over their unruly emotions. As we have seen, the Stoics are particularly adamant in their condemnation of anger in its "raw" and unfettered forms. On the other hand, as Prof. Nancy Sherman has pointed out in her book, *Stoic Warriors*, there is a role for carefully modulated anger, *when the stakes are worthy of our moral indignation.* She gives, as one example, the experience of U.S. Army warrant officer, Hugh Thomson, at the infamous My Lai massacre of the Vietnam conflict. Thomson, acting in part from a sense of moral outrage, had his crew train their guns on American soldiers who were slaughtering civilians, and was able to mitigate the massacre. But this kind of carefully-channeled outrage is a far cry from the unmitigated rage we saw in the case of Felicity.

As Aristotle shrewdly observed, our aim ought to be, ". . . to be angry with the right person and to the right degree and at the right time and for the right purpose, and in the right way." To be sure, this is no easy task, and the Rabbis of the Talmud observed that even God has exceedingly brief moments of anger! And yet, as the Buddhist sages have counseled, we may gradually learn to modulate, if not eliminate our anger, through patience, self-examination, and a willingness to investigate the supposed causes of our anger. As Thich Nhat Hanh puts it,

> "While embracing your anger, you [should] practice
> looking deeply to see the nature of your anger,
> because you know that you may be the victim of
> a wrong perception. You may have misunderstood
> what you heard and saw. You may have a wrong
> idea of what had been said, what had been done . . .
> You yourself may have created the hell inside you."
> (*Anger: Wisdom for Cooling the Flames*, p. 59)

**Sadly, Seneca was apparently not a great friend of the Jews; on the contrary, he reflected the same animosity toward the Jews as his Roman contemporaries, once referring to the Jews as "that most accursed nation." And yet, in many other ways, Seneca was a decent and principled man—at least, much of his writing reflects the high value he put on compassion toward others.

Chapter 10

SUMMING UP

I began this book by proposing that ". . . the synthesis of Judaism, Buddhism, and Stoicism can create a healthy, fulfilled and flourishing life." Have I succeeded in demonstrating this? I suspect that any such demonstration must await the transformative efforts of my readers, over many months or years. Only by deliberate and persistent effort can the principles outlined in this book be woven into the emotional life of the reader. But perhaps it will help to review the main themes we have been exploring, by way of drawing out a few key lessons.

First, we discussed a theme common to all three of our traditions; namely, that our happiness and fulfillment in life is critically dependent on *the quality of our thinking*. We suggested that, in effect, we create our own happiness by thinking "good" thoughts—and create our own misery by filling our minds with "bad" thoughts. More specifically, Judaism emphasizes *rational understanding*, without which we are spiritually and emotionally "lost". Thus, we cited the Talmudic teaching of Rabbi Elazar that, ". . . any person who lacks understanding eventually goes into exile . . ." Similarly, the Buddhist text, the *Dhammapada* teaches us that "We are what we think . . . with our thoughts we make the world." We also cited the Thai Buddhist Master, Ajahn Chah (1918-92) as saying,

> "We want to be free of suffering . . . but still we
> suffer. Why is this? It's because of wrong thinking. If
> our thinking is in harmony with the way things are,
> we will have well-being."

In the Stoic tradition, too, we find pride of place given to *thinking clearly.* Epictetus reminds us that, "It is not he who gives abuse . . . who offends us; but the view that we take of these things as insulting or hurtful . . ." and urges us ". . . . not to be bewildered by appearances."

Moreover, all three spiritual paths emphasize that we often sabotage our chances for living the "good life" through our own distorted thinking. Echoing the views of many modern cognitive-behavioral therapists, Rabbi Dr. Joseph Gelberman tells us that, "Of all the tyrants in the world, our own attitudes are the fiercest warlords." Similarly, the Buddhist monk, Chagdud Tulku teaches that, "Hell is the reflection of [the] mind's delusion, of angry thoughts and intentions and the harmful words and actions they produce." He adds—once again sounding much like our modern cognitive therapists—"It's our failure to understand the essential nature of an emotion as it arises that gets us into trouble. Once we do, the emotion tends to dissolve." Indeed, we are often our own worst enemies, as the great Buddhist sage, Santideva (7th c. AD), put it: "Eager to escape sorrow, men rush into sorrow; from desire of happiness, they blindly slay their own happiness, enemies to themselves."

We went on to discuss "the common bond of humanity" as an idea central to all three of our traditions. Thus, Judaism teaches us that we are all created "in the Divine image", and that, as Rabbi Moseh Lieber puts it,

> ". . . we must treat people properly because all people
> play a role in God's plans; nobody was created for

naught, be it a fool, an ignoramus, or even an evil
person. They are all part of the Divine Scheme . . ."

Similarly, Buddhism emphasizes the essential unity of
mankind, and, indeed, all sentient beings. This attitude is
expressed in the concepts of *Buddha nature, suffering,* and
compassion. As Wallace puts it, ". . . all sentient beings, including
humans, are endowed with Buddha-nature . . . [defined as] the
potential for full awakening . . ." All human beings experience
suffering (*dukha*), and thereby have the opportunity—indeed,
the obligation—to cultivate compassion for every other human
being. This concept is also stressed in Stoicism, and is given a
rather spiritualized treatment in the writings of Marcus Aurelius's
Meditations:

> "All things are woven together and the common
> bond is sacred . . . for there is one Universe out of
> all, one God through all, one substance and one law,
> one common Reason of all intelligent creatures, and
> one truth . . ."

The importance of *moral obligations* appears as a prominent
theme in all three traditions, and is intimately connected with
the achievement of a "flourishing life." That is, living ethically is
not merely an obligation; it is also a kind of portal into the realm
of *self-realization*. To put it in more colloquial terms, if you live
ethically, you will live well and fully. Thus, the Talmud teaches
us that "The reward of a good deed is a good deed"—in effect,
behaving ethically is its own reward. Furthermore, as Rabbi
Alexander Ziskin observes, fulfilling a commandment ". . . is a
time to feel great joy at your relationship with God."

You may recall that among the elements of Buddhism's
"Eightfold Path" are *right speech, right conduct,* and *right vocation,*

all considered under the rubric of *sila* (the code of conduct that leads to virtue). *Sila,* in turn, is the key to living the fulfilled life, according to Buddhist teachings. As B. Allen Wallace succinctly puts it, "The Buddhist view is simple: non-virtuous behavior leads to misery: virtuous behavior leads to joy." The Tibetan Buddhist nun, Thubten Chodron defined the essence of the Buddha's teachings with equal brevity: ". . . it is to avoid harming others and to help them as much as possible."

For the Stoics, too, the key to living "the good life" lies in living the *morally responsible* life. Every other notion of "the good" proves to be illusory. Thus, Seneca writes in one of his letters, "A good character is the only guarantee of everlasting, carefree happiness." Similarly, Epictetus argues that "The good for human beings lies in this one thing alone: for each of us to perfect our moral character . . ." In sum, the JuBuSto tradition emphasizes that only by living ethical lives can we achieve genuine happiness and become fully human.

All three of our traditions stress the importance of reducing, or modulating, what we have termed "desires and attachments." While none of the traditions argues for the total elimination of desires, each admonishes us to "detach" ourselves from intense and overwhelming cravings. From the Jewish perspective, probably nobody has put the matter more clearly than Maimonides, in *The Guide for the Perplexed*: "All the difficulties and troubles we meet [in daily life] are due to the desire for superfluous things . . . the more we desire to have the superfluous, the more we meet with difficulties."

Maimonides the rationalist is joined by Nahman of Bratslav, the mystic, in pointing to the dangers of excessive attachments and desires. Nahman tells us that, "Worldly desires are like sunbeams in a dark room. They may seem solid, but the person who tries to grasp a sunbeam finds nothing in his hand. The same is true of all worldly desires."

The Buddhist tradition is, if anything, even more focused than the rabbis on the dangers of "grasping onto things" (*upadana*). As Ajahn Chah puts it, "The extraordinary suffering is the suffering that arises from what we call *upadana*, grasping on to things. This is like [receiving] an injection with a syringe filled with poison." At the same time—and in this, the rabbis would concur—Buddhism teaches that there's nothing inherently wrong in enjoying life's pleasures, or even indulging in an occasional luxury. In fact, as Tibetan Buddhist nun, *Thubten Chodron*, points out, ". . . it's attachment that makes us restless and prevents us from enjoying things." In effect, we become so fixated on the object of our attachment that we can barely appreciate it.

Buddhism goes on to teach us that the way to reduce excessive attachment is by realizing the *impermanence* of everything—including, of course, our own lives. As Aitken Roshi tells us, "Renunciation is not getting rid of the things of this world, but *accepting that they pass away.*" (italics added)

The Stoics, too, emphasize simplicity, lack of pretension, and non-attachment to fame, fortune and status symbols. For the Stoics, the only real "good" in life is *virtue*. As Marcus Aurelius so eloquently puts it, "There is but one thing of real value—to cultivate truth and justice, and to live without anger in the midst of lying and unjust men." It follows, then, that acquiring possessions, wealth, honor, prestige, and influence are merely illusory goods. But like the rabbis and the Buddhist sages, it is not "things in themselves" that are judged unworthy of the fully-developed person; rather, it is our intense attachment to these things. Thus, in describing his father, Marcus Aurelius writes,

> "My father enjoyed, without pretention or self-indulgence, the luxuries that his fortune lavished upon him; but when these were not available, he

never seemed to miss them." (from The Emperor's Handbook, 1.23).

We next discussed the attitude of the three traditions toward *impermanence and mortality*. All three recognize that our earthly existence is alarmingly short (though a proper understanding of life might lead us to be far less "alarmed"). In the Jewish tradition, we are put here on earth in order to refine our moral character and serve God. As Rabbi Moshe Lieber teaches us, "Life is a fleeting opportunity to gather [spiritual] treasure; once the time is up, [one] can no longer earn anything." Given that we never know when our "time is up," we must treat every day as if it were our last. Thus, as Rabbi Lieber puts it, the righteous person ". . . must always assume that today is the last day of his life and not push off his repentance. Hence, he will spend all his life in perpetual self-improvement." Similarly, Rabbi Abraham Joshua Heschel teaches us that, "Life's ultimate meaning remains obscure unless it is reflected upon in the face of death . . . [Judaism's] central concern is not how to escape death but rather, how to sanctify life."

This teaching is very close in spirit to the Buddhist teaching in the *Dhammapada:*

> "Neither father, sons nor one's relations can stop the King of Death . . . [One] who is virtuous and wise understands the meaning of this, and swiftly strives with all his might to clear a path to Nirvana."

Buddhism, however, takes a somewhat different attitude than Judaism when it comes to placing value on our earthly existence. Whereas in Judaism, life is sanctified and valued as an opportunity to perfect ourselves in God's ways, Buddhism sees earthly existence in more detached terms—not fundamentally different than other things governed by *anicca* (impermanence). Thus, Ajahn Chah writes,

> "Suppose you were sick and had to go into the hospital. Most people think, "Please don't let me die, I want to get better." That is wrong thinking, [and] it will lead to suffering. You have to think to yourself, "If I recover, I recover, if I die, I die." This is right thinking . . ."

Though this is not the typical attitude of Judaism—at least in modern times—we noted a similar sentiment in the *viduy* prayer in Judaism, said when the person is near death; i.e., the righteous Jew says to God, "*May it be Your will to heal me. But if death is my lot, then I accept it from Your hand with love.*"

Thus, both Judaism and Buddhism share with Stoicism a certain reserve toward earthly existence, as expressed by Marcus Aurelius: "[T]he one who lives longest and the one who will die soonest lose just the same." But for Marcus, as for the rabbis and Buddhist sages, this equanimity does not relieve us of our ethical responsibilities. Marcus admonishes us, "Since it is possible that you may depart from life this very moment, regard every act and thought accordingly." By this, Marcus means that we must live honorably, reasonably, and in accordance with Nature, at all times. He cautions us, "Don't act as though you'll live to be a thousand . . . in what remains of your allotted time, while you still can, become good." (*The Emperor's Handbook,* 4.17).

Seneca sums up the Stoic view of mortality when he writes, "The man whom you should admire and imitate is the one who finds it a joy to live, and in spite of that, is not reluctant to die."

We went on to explore the importance of *gratitude* in the three traditions, and found that each places great importance on this quality of mind. In the Talmudic tradition, gratitude is expressed for whatever one has been allotted in life, as when Ben Zoma asks, "Who is rich?" and replies, "One who rejoices in one's portion." Perhaps reflecting a much earlier Stoic teaching, the 13th century sage, Jacob Anatoli taught that, "If a man cannot get what he wants, he ought to want what he can get." (Toperoff 1997, 197). In the Jewish tradition, it is impossible to conceive of "the flourishing life" without the capacity to feel thankfulness and gratitude. We cited the Yiddish proverb about being grateful—if you break a leg—that you didn't break both legs! Or, as a cartoon by Mankoff in the *New Yorker* put it—showing a woman standing next to her worried-looking husband—"But why not be happy about all the diseases that you *don't* have?"

In Buddhism, too, gratitude (*katannuta*) is a foundational virtue. This is summed up in the saying attributed to the Buddha: "Let us rise up and be thankful, for if we didn't learn a lot today, at least we learned a little; and if we didn't learn a little, at least we didn't get sick; and if we got sick, at least we didn't die; so let us all be thankful." And, as Phillip Moffit observes, gratitude yields additional rewards. It becomes part of a "virtuous cycle" and is an integral part of the flourishing life: "Cultivating thankfulness for being part of life blossoms into a feeling of being blessed, not in the sense of winning the lottery, but in a more refined appreciation for the interdependent nature of life. It also elicits feelings of generosity, which create further joy . . ."

For the Stoics, gratitude is summed up in Seneca's teaching, which sounds remarkably like Jacob Anatoli's comment: "It is in no man's power to have whatever he wants; but he has it in his power not to wish for what he hasn't got, and cheerfully make the most of the things that do come his way." And, we took note of Cicero's gratitude, in the midst of his old age, for the ". . . supreme satisfaction to be derived from an old age which has knowledge and learning to feed upon . . ."

Finally, we explored the foundational value of *self-restraint*, and in particular, the necessity of controlling our anger. All three of our traditions would concur in arguing that no one who seeks a flourishing life can give vent to uncontrolled anger—at least, not on a recurring basis. The rabbinical tradition emphasizes the virtue of being *slow to anger*, and recognizes that the total elimination of all angry feelings is virtually impossible for all but a few saints and sages—and some sages doubt that such eradication of anger would be entirely a good thing. The rabbis also recognized the element of *narcissism* in unbridled anger, which is compared to "worshipping idols." Similarly, in the *Dhammapada*, the Buddhist tradition holds that,

> "A man is not on the path of righteousness if he settles
> matters in a violent haste. A wise man calmly considers
> what is right and what is wrong, and faces different
> opinions with truth, non-violence, and peace."

Buddhism holds that *patience* is the antidote to anger and aggression, and urges us to look deeply within ourselves to find the real cause of our anger. As Thich Nhat Hanh observes, "You yourself may have created the hell inside you."

The Stoics, too, saw intense anger as a genuine evil—even one that could "beget madness," as Epicurus put it. Furthermore, the one who is overcome by anger forgets important truths about our place in the overall order of things. As Marcus Aurelius observes, "I cannot be angry with a brother or resent him, for we were born into this world to work together like the feet, hands, eyelids and lower rows of teeth . . ." Moreover, "Whenever you lose your temper or become upset about something . . . you're forgetting that everything is what your opinion makes it, and that the present moment is all you have, to live and lose."

*   *   *

Afterword

In this book, I have emphasized the common threads that run through the tapestry of three great spiritual traditions. In many respects, I find more similarities than differences in the way Judaism, Buddhism and Stoicism have come to understand "the flourishing life"—what the Greeks called *eudaimonia*. Yet it would be a mistake to regard the underlying premises of these traditions as interchangeable, much less identical. There are important differences that we have not discussed, particularly with respect to Judaism and Buddhism. To put the matter crudely (and somewhat inaccurately), traditional Judaism posits an omnipotent and omniscient Creator, whose divine commandments and teachings we must honor—in short, traditional Judaism is founded on *man's relationship with, and responsibilities to, God.*

In general, Buddhism has no corresponding principle identifying a single "Godhead" with the creation or moral order of the universe. And whereas we find numerous references to "the gods"—and even to "God"—in Stoic philosophy, no teachings attributed to the Buddha specifically mention God in the sense used by the Abrahamic faiths (Judaism, Christianity, and Islam). There are many other differences between Judaism and Buddhism, and the interested reader may consult the book, *Letters to a Buddhist Jew*, in which David Gottlieb—who identifies himself as a "Zen Jew struggling to resolve these two identities"—poses a series of key questions to Rabbi Akiva Tatz. Similarly, Stoicism and Judaism have important historical and philosophical points of intersection; yet few would argue that they are fundamentally alike in their underlying metaphysical or theological premises.

In very rudimentary terms, I would suggest that both Stoicism and Buddhism are essentially philosophical and cognitive in nature; they direct us toward certain concepts, attitudes, and perspectives that do not require a personal relationship with an omniscient and omnipotent God. Judaism, notwithstanding its profound philosophical underpinnings, is much more concerned with man's *sacred and covenantal relationship with God*—an eternal and ineffable being who not only created the universe, but who also cares deeply about mankind. Indeed, in the more mystical and "kabbalistic" strains of Judaism, *God depends on man* to help restore the moral order of the universe—a task sometimes subsumed in the term, *tikkun olam* (roughly, "repairing the world"). One mystical saying in Judaism is that "Man upholds the heavens"—signifying that the celestial order cannot be maintained without righteous acts on the part of mankind. It's fair to say that neither Buddhism nor Stoicism places man in such a crucial and intimate moral relationship with the Creator.

Notwithstanding these numerous differences, I hope that by now, the reader is persuaded that Judaism, Buddhism, and Stoicism share many of the same beliefs, as regards "the good life" and how we can attain it. I believe that these beliefs are relatively autonomous; that is, they stand largely apart from whatever metaphysical or theological assumptions underlie the three traditions. Indeed, I believe that we can harmonize and integrate many of the teachings of these traditions, without necessarily endorsing their metaphysical underpinnings. Though many in the "orthodox" communities of the three faiths may disagree, I believe that we can live ethically and fruitfully without necessarily believing in the God of the Hebrew Bible; the Buddhist concept of *samsara;* or the Stoic *logos*. We can achieve the flourishing life by embracing the core values that underlie Judaism, Buddhism and Stoicism: respect for all sentient life; reasoned judgment in all things; moderation in all actions; and above all, kindness toward all our fellow human beings.

Lexington, MA
December, 2012

References and Sources

Ajahn Chah, Breiter P: *Everything arises, everything falls away*. Shambhala, 2005.

Ajahn Chah: *Living Dhamma*, The Sangha (1992)

Anonymous. *The Dhammapada: The Path of Perfection*. Translated by Juan Mascaro. Penguin Classics, 1973

Aurelius M: *Marcus Aurelius: Meditations*. Trans. A.S.L. Farquharson. New York, Knopf, Everyman's Library, 1946.

Aurelius M: *The Emperor's Handbook*. Translated by C. Scot Hicks and David V. Hicks. Scribner, 2002.

Aurelius M: *The Meditations of Marcus Aurelius*. Trans. G. Long. Boston, Shambhala, 1993.

Bancroft A: *The Buddha Speaks: A Book of Guidance from the Buddhist Scriptures*. Shambhala, 2000

Baron JL (editor): *A Treasury of Jewish Quotations*, Jason Aronson Inc., 1996

Batchelor S: *Buddhism Without Beliefs: A Contemporary Guide to Awakening*, Riverhead Trade, 1998

Becker E: *The Denial of Death*. Free Press, 1975

Bemporad J: *The Inner Journey. Views from the Jewish Tradition*. Morning Light Press, 2007

Besserman P, *The Way of the Jewish Mystics,* Shambhala 1994.

Bonforte J: *The Philosophy of Epictetus*. New York, Philosophical Library, 1955

Borowitz EB, Schwartz FW: *The Jewish Moral Virtues*. Jewish Publication Society, 1999.

Bulka R, *Chapters of the Sages*, <u>A Psychological Commentary on Pirkey Avoth</u>, Jason Aronson, 1977

Bunim IM: *Ethics from Sinai*. Feldheim, 1964

Burtt EA: *The Teachings of the Compassionate Buddha*, Mentor, 1982

Chagdud Tulku: *Gates to Buddhist Practice: Essential Teachings of a Tibetan Master*. Padma Publishing, 2001

Chodron T: *Buddhism for Beginners*, Snow Lion Publications, 2001

Cicero. *On Old Age,* translated by E. S. Shuckburgh. Vol. IX, Part 2. The Harvard Classics. New York: P.F. Collier & Son, 1909-14; Bartleby.com, 2001. <u>www.bartleby.com/9/2/</u>.

Cicero: *Selected Works*. Transl. by Michael Grant, Penguin, 1971

Cohen H: "Peace and Death." In: *Contemporary Jewish Thought*. Edited by S. Noveck, Bnai Brith Books, 1985

Comte-Sponville A: *A Small Treatise on the Great Virtues: The Uses of Philosophy in Everyday Life.* Picador; 2002

Dan J: *The Teachings of Hasidism*, Behrman House, 1984.

Davis C: *Greek and Roman Stoicism*. Boston, Herbert B. Turner & Co., 1903

De botton A: *The Consolations of Philosophy*, Vintage, 2001

Dorff E: *The Way into Tikkun Olam: Repairing the world.* Jewish Lights Publishing, 2005

Ellis A, Harper R: *A Guide to Rational Living,* Melvin Powers/Wilshire Book Co., 1961

Finkel AY: *Ein Yaakov: The Ethical and Inspirational Teachings of the Talmud.* Jason Aronson, 1999

Gewirtz LB: *The authentic Jew and his Judaism: An analysis of the basic concepts of the Jewish religion.* Bloch Pub. Co, 1961

Gribetz J: *Wise Words: Jewish Thoughts and Stories Through the Ages.* Harper Perennial, 2004

Guttman J: *Philosophies of Judaism: The History of Jewish Philosophy from Biblical Times to Franz Rosenzweig.* Schocken Books, 1973

Hayim H. Donin *To Be A Jew* Basic Books, 1991

Irvine W: *A Guide to the Good Life: The Ancient Art of Stoic Joy*, Oxford University Press, 2008.

Jacobs L: *Concise Companion to the Jewish Religion.* Oxford University Press, 1999

Jacobson S: *Toward a Meaningful Life, New Edition: The Wisdom of the Rebbe Menachem Mendel Schneerson.* William Morrow, 2002.

Kamenetz R: *The Jew in the Lotus. A Poet's Rediscovery of Jewish Identity in Buddhist India.* Harper One, 2007.

Kanfer S: *The Essential Groucho: Writings For By And About Groucho Marx*, Vintage, 2000.

Lankevich GL: *The Wit & Wisdom of the Talmud: Proverbs, Sayings, and Parables for the Ages.* Square One Publishers, 2003

Lieber M: *Pirke Avos Treasury.* Edited by N. Scherman. Brooklyn, Mesorah Publications, 1995.

McGuckin JA: *The Westminster Handbook to Patristic Theology*, Westminster John Knox Press, 2004

Nissenson H: *The Elephant and My Jewish Problem: Short Stories and Journals*, 1957-1987. Harpercollins, 1988

Oates WJ: *The Stoic and Epicurean Philosophers: The Complete Extant Writings of Epicurus, Epictetus, Lucretius, Marcus Aurelius*, Modern Library edition, 1949

Pali-English Dictionary, edited by T.W.R. Davids, W. Stede. Motilal Banarsidass Publ., 1993

Pies R: *Everything Has Two Handles: The Stoic's Guide to the Art of Living*. Hamilton Books, 2008

Prothero S: "Religions of the East" (lectures). Modern Scholar Series, Recorded Books, 2005.

Robertson D: *The Philosophy of Cognitive Behavioural Therapy: Stoic Philosophy as Rational and Cognitive Psychotherapy*, Karnac Books, 2010

Roth D: *Relevance: Pirke Avos for the Twenty-First century*. Feldheim, 2007

Seddon K: *Epictetus' Handbook and the Tablet of Cebes: Guides to Stoic Living*, Taylor & Francis, 2007

Seneca: *Letters from a Stoic*. Transl. by Robin Campbell, Penguin Books, 1969

Shantideva: *The Bodhicaryavatara* (Oxford World's Classics) Paul Williams, Kate Crosby and Andrew Skilton (editors/translators) Oxford University Press, 2008.

Sherman N: *Stoic Warriors: The Ancient Philosophy behind the Military Mind*. Oxford University Press, 2007

Sherwin BL, Cohen SJ, *Creating an Ethical Jewish Life*. Jewish Lights, 2001.

Silver YI: The Code of Jewish Conduct. Israel Book Shop, 2008 Accessed at: http://www.hebrewpublishing.com/pdf/Mishpete_Hashalom_complete.pdf

Snelling J: *The Buddhist Handbook: A Complete Guide to Buddhist Schools, Teaching, Practice, and History*

Steinsaltz A: *The Three-Petalled Rose.*

Telushkin J: *Hillel: If Not Now, When?* Jewish Encounters, 2010

Telushkin J: *The Book of Jewish Values*, Harmony Books, 2000.

Telushkin J: *A Code of Jewish Ethics*, vol. 1, Harmony, 2006

Teshima JY: *Zen Buddhism and Hasidism*, University Press of America, 1995

Thich Nhat Hanh: *Living Buddha*, Living Christ

Thich Nhat Hanh, *The Heart of the Buddha's Teaching: Transforming Suffering into Peace, Joy, and Liberation*

Thich Nhat Hanh: *Anger: Wisdom for Cooling the Flame.* Riverhead Trade, 2002

Thurman R: *Infinite Life: Awakening to Bliss Within.* Riverhead Trade, 2005

Tirosh-Samuelson H: *Happiness in Premodern Judaism: Virtue, Knowledge, and Well-Being* (Monographs of the Hebrew Union College) 2003

Toperoff S: *Avot.* Jason Aronson, 1997

Twersky I: *A Maimonides Reader.* Library of Jewish Studies, Berhman House, 1972

Unger F. (editor): Goethe's World View, Frederick Ungar Publishing; 1963

Ven. Lobsang Gyatso: *Bodhichitta: Cultivating the Compassionate Mind of Enlightenment*, accessed at: http://tinyplace.org/tinyblog/archives/2001/03/the_shortcomings_of_the_selfcentered_attitude.php

Walden M.M (ed.): *Niflaot ha-Rebbe*, Bnei Brak, Israel

Wallace BA, Wilhelm S: *Tibetan Buddhism from the Ground Up: A Practical Approach for Modern Life*, Wisdom Publications, 1993

Watts AW: *The Way of Zen*. Vintage Books, 1957

Weiss RL, Butterworth CE: *Ethical Writings of Maimonides*. New York University Press (1975)

Yalom I:. *Staring at the Sun: Overcoming the Terror of Death* Jossey-Bass, 2009.

Glossary of Terms

Judaism

Aggadah (or Hagaddah)—non-legal material in the Talmud, including moral aphorisms and folklore

emunah—faith, faithfulness, trustworthiness

erekh apayim—slow to anger

Gemara—Commentary on the *Mishnah*

Halacha—Jewish law; the legal material in the Talmud

Hasidism—the Jewish mystical tradition, emphasizing joy and direct experience of God

Lashon hara—literally, "the evil tongue"; more technically, any *true* statement that reduces the stature of the person about whom it is said

Mishnah—the first portion of the Talmud, as established under the *Tannaim* (ca. 70-200 CE).

Mitzvah—a commandment or rabbinical directive; more loosely, an act of kindness *motzi shem ra*—literally, "giving another a bad name;" more technically, derogatory *and false* statements about someone [cf. *lashon hara*]

Pirkei Avot—The only major section of the Talmud (*Mishna*) dealing exclusively with ethical teachings and maxims (*Aggadah*)

Rahamim—the quality of kindness and compassion

shalom bayit—literally, "peace at home"; household harmony

Talmud—compilation of rabbinical commentaries on the Torah, consisting of the *Mishnah* and the *Gemara*.

Tanakh—the five books of Moses; eight books of the *prophets*; and the eleven books of *writings*, constituting the Hebrew Bible.

Torah—literally, "instruction"; often translated as "law"; the five books of Moses in the Hebrew Bible. More broadly, the entire body of ethical "instruction" that guides the Jewish people

tzedakah—often defined as "charity", but more accurately: acting justly (from *tzedek*, meaning "justice").

yetzer hara—the "evil inclination"

yetzer hatov—the "good inclination"

yishuv hadaat—a calm, settled state of mind (from *yashav*, meaning *to sit*)

Buddhism

Akatannuta—ingratitude

alobha—non-attachment

Amitabha—the "Buddha of Infinite Light" in Pure Land school [see appendix]

anicca—impermanence, uncertainty

arhat—in Theravada Buddhism, the perfected disciple

Avalokiteshvara—the bodhisattva of compassion

bodhicitta—a state of mental enlightenment

bodhisattva—one who seeks *bodhicitta*; i.e., one who defers entrance into *nirvana* in order to liberate others

Buddha—The Illumined or Enlightened One; the founder of Buddhism.

Buddha nature—the capacity to "wake up" and become enlightened, inherent in all of us

dhamma (Dharma)—the collective teachings of the Buddha; the way of truth

dukkha—unsatisfactoriness, the suffering inherent in existence *karma*—the impersonal, causal principle working itself out via retributive justice; "what you put into the universe, you will ultimately get back."

katannuta—gratitude

koan—paradoxical statement aimed at jolting the student into new understanding

Lotus school—Mahayana sect, also called *Tendai,* focuses on *Lotus Sutra*

Lotus sutra—key text in Mahayana Buddhism, introduces *Avalokiteshvara*

Mahayana—"Greater Vehicle"; Buddhist school stressing the role of the *bodhisattva*

moksha—release of the soul from the cycle of *samsara*

Nicheren—form of Japanese Buddhism emphasizing recitation of the mantra *namu myoho renge kyo* ("salutation to the Lotus Sutra").

nirvana—the enlightened state in which desire and aversion are extinguished

paramita—perfection, ideal virtue

Pure Land—Mahayana sect, believes Nirvana no longer possible to attain; focuses on devotion to *Amitabha (Amida) Buddha*

samadhi—complete concentration, focus

samsara—the eternal cycle of birth, death, and rebirth

Sangha—the community of those who follow the Buddha's way

Shakyamuni—Siddhartha Gautama, the Buddha (ca. 560 BCE to 480 BCE)

sila-morality, conduct in accord with virtue

tanha—"blind demandingness"; asking more of the world than it can provide

Tantra—concept of transmuting desire in order to foster spiritual progress

upādāna—attachment, clinging, grasping onto things (lit., "fuel")

Theravada—"Way of the Elders"; major division of Buddhism emphasizing monastic discipline; also called Hinayana

triratna: "The Three Jewels" (the *Buddha*, the *Dhamma*, and the *Sangha)*

Vajrayana—Tibetan Buddhism

vipassana—lit., "special seeing"; insight meditation

Zen—means "meditation; one of many Mahayana schools, strongly influenced by Daoism; focuses on attaining enlightenment through meditation. *Soto Zen* emphasizes "sitting meditation" (*zazen*); *Rinzai Zen* emphasizes use of the *koan* (paradox)

Stoicism

apatheia—equanimity of spirit

eudaimonia—often translated as "happiness", but really connoting a state in which one uses one's rational faculties in accordance with virtue, thus achieving a "flourishing life."

euroia biou—the "good flow" of life

Logos—the principle of cosmic order and rationality, or reason, sometimes identified with Nature or God

Appendix:
Buddhism divisions and beliefs

Main Divisions, Sects & Schools	Key Beliefs/ Practices/Texts	Notes
Theravada	"Way of the Elders" (also called Hinayana); authoritative text is the Pali Canon; purpose of life is to become an *arhat*, a perfected saint who has achieved nirvana and will not be reborn again. Believes it unlikely that a layperson can achieve liberation; tends to be more monastic, strict and world-renouncing than Mahayana. Rituals are not emphasized.	"Southern" school, flourishes in Ceylon, Burma, Thailand. Only one surviving school of original 18

Mahayana	More "liberal," accessible school of Buddhism. As "Greater Vehicle" (literally, the "Greater Ox-Cart"), Mahayana is path available to all, not just monks. Goal is not to become *arhats* but *boddhisatvas*, enlightened saints who delay achieving nirvana to help others attain it. Recognizes many Buddhas of many eras. Accepts the Pali canon, but also the *Sutras*, later Sanskrit texts. Numerous rituals. Has *four main sects* [below], three of which revere the **Lotus Sutra***.	"Northern Buddhism", mainly in China, Japan, Korea. ***Lotus Sutra** is composed of parables; teaches that all beings may attain buddhahood and attain Nirvana. Presents itself as true and complete teaching of the Buddha, who is described as transcendent eternal being. Lotus Sutra introduces *Avalokiteśvara*, the Bodhisattva of compassion who assists those in distress.
Nicheren	Form of Japanese Buddhism that emphasizes repeated recitation of the mantra *namu myoho renge kyo* ("salutation to the **Lotus Sutra**"). Nichiren Buddhists believe enlightenment can be attained in a single lifetime, via prolonged recitation of mantra and other practices.	Named for founder, Japanese monk, Nichiren Daishonin (1222-1282). Very critical of other forms of Buddhism; sees Nicheren as only correct school. *Soka Gakkai International* (SGI) is the umbrella organization for affiliate lay organizations; some (perhaps unfairly) claim SGI is "cult".

Pure Land	Believes Nirvana no longer possible to attain; one should focus on **devotion to Amitabha (Amida)**, which will gain one enough karmic merit to go to "Pure Land" (heavenly paradise). Frequent chanting mantra of devotion to Amida, "Namu Amida Butsu," to foster sincerity and gain admission to the Pure Land, at death. **Lotus Sutra** also important.	**Amitabha** is one of 5 "Wisdom Buddahs", and is Buddha of Infinite Light
Tendai (tien tai)	Doctrines and practices similar to Zen and based on **Lotus Sutra**. Also incorporates some elements of Shinto, the indigenous Japanese tradition.	Sometimes known as the **Lotus School;** largest school of Buddhism; has had great influence on Chinese and Japanese society.
Zen	"Zen" means "meditation." It focuses on attaining enlightenment (*bodhi,* or "waking up") through meditation; teaches that all human beings embody the Buddha-nature & potential to attain enlightenment; but Buddha-nature has been clouded by ignorance. Rejects study of scriptures, religious rites, devotional practices, and good works; fosters meditation leading to sudden flash of insight, and awareness of ultimate reality.	Strongly influenced by Daoism; training in Zen path usually undertaken by a disciple under guidance of a master.
Soto	Emphasizes *zazen*, or sitting meditation, as the means to attain enlightenment	Arrived in Japan in 1227 upon the teacher Dogen's return from China

Rinzai	Emphasizes use of *koans*, paradoxical puzzles or questions that help the practitioner overcome conventional logic	Introduced to Japan by the Chinese priest Ensai in 1191
Vajrayana (Tibetan)	Like Mahayana schools, Tibetan Buddhism recognizes many Buddhas & bodhisattvas; meditation is an important function which may be aided by the use of special hand gestures (*mudras*) and chanted *mantras* (e.g., mantra of Avalokiteshvara: "*om mani padme hum*"). Highly "syncretic"; i.e., Tibetan Buddhism incorporates *Tantric* symbolic rituals, Theravadin monastic discipline, shamanistic features. Most famous Tibetan Buddhist text is the ***Bardo Thodol***, popularly known as the ***Tibetan Book of the Dead.***	Origin in arrival of the great tantric mystic, ***Padmasambhava*** in Tibet in **774 CE;** well-known today through the Dalai Lama, the exiled spiritual and political leader of Tibet. The *Bardo Thodol* ("Liberation through hearing in the intermediate state") is a funerary text that describes experiences of the soul during the interval between death and rebirth (called *bardo*). Tantric rituals may originally have involved sexual acts by monks; in modern times, these are visualized or "imagined."

Main reference: http://www.religionfacts.com/buddhism/sects.htm; lecture notes from Prof. Stephen Prothero, Boston University (Religions of the East (lectures). Modern Scholar Series, Recorded Books, 2005.)

About the Author

Ronald Pies MD, is Professor of Psychiatry and Lecturer on Bioethics & Humanities at SUNY Upstate Medical University in Syracuse; and Clinical Professor of Psychiatry at Tufts in Boston. He is author or editor of a number of psychiatric textbooks, as well as a collection of short stories (*Ziprin's Ghost* Harvard Book Store) and of poetry (*Creeping Thyme*/Brandylane; *The Heart Broken Open*/Paige Guttenborg). Dr. Pies has written extensively in the areas of Judaic studies, comparative religion, and philosophy. His most recent books, include *The Judaic Foundations of Cognitive-Behavioral Therapy: Rabbinical and Talmudic Underpinnings of CBT and REBT* (iUniverse); *Everything Has Two Handles: The Stoic's Guide to the Art of Living* (Hamilton Books); and *Becoming a Mensch*, also from Hamilton Books. Dr. Pies has been a contributor to *The New York Times*, the *Boston Globe*, and numerous literary journals, including *The Bellevue Literary Review*, *Creative Nonfiction*, and *The Healing Muse*. His poems have appeared in several anthologies. Dr. Pies and his wife, Nancy, live outside of Boston.